PHOTOGRAPHIC MEMORY

ADVANCED TECHNIQUES TO IMPROVE YOUR MEMORY, REMEMBER MORE, LEARN QUICKLY, AND INCREASE PRODUCTIVITY AS STUDENTS, LAWYER, ACCOUNTANT ETC.

ALAN O'BRIEN

of information contained in this document, including, but not limited to, - errors, omissions, or inaccuracies.

TABLE OF CONTENTS

INTRODUCTION

Before we get started, I would like to thank you and congratulate you for downloading and reading this book!

Let me ask you a question. Do you ever feel too stressed out from all the responsibilities and duties you need to carry out? Do you ever feel too overwhelmed by the sheer pressures of life? Are you too busy with all the countless things you need to get done? Are you too distracted to focus and get the things needed to be done? Do you often get sidetracked and forget all the things you need to get started on? A good memory is a must-have skill to make your life easier and to improve your productivity. It can also improve your chances of success in most fields including, teachers, translators, students, accountants, in job interviews, finishing a project, giving a speech, connecting with people, and much more. The likelihood of success in such fields will increase drastically if you can develop an extraordinarily good memory. Luckily for you, in this very book, you can improve your memory with all the techniques and useful advice this book contains. As a matter of fact, a number of people have shown significant improvement in their memory after utilizing these techniques and tips.

In this book, you will learn all about memory which can drastically help you become more efficient in your studies, your personal life, and in your professional life. You will learn many memory methods and tips to maximize your productivity, learn faster, and to achieve greater success. Memory improvement is a necessary skill in life. The more things you remember, the less stress and easier your life becomes. Learning will become swift, and it will be easier for you to apply this newfound knowledge to improve your life. This book puts an enormous importance on your ability to remember, learn, and make use of valuable information in your everyday lives.

This book is an all-inclusive memory book which offers some of the best and proven memory techniques, an understanding of remembrance, and much advice and helpful information to reach maximum memory. Also, you can read this book in any order you want. If you need to learn a specific skill, you can easily navigate it through the 'Table of Contents.' In any case, I am positive that this book will help you tremendously.

Thanks again for downloading this book, I really hope that you enjoy it! With all that being said, let's get started!

CHAPTER 1: UNDERSTANDING HOW MEMORY WORKS

Before we can begin to partake into the techniques of memory improvement, we must comprehend how memory functions. It is important not to overlook this chapter because different techniques will correlate with the memory in a variety of ways.

WHAT IS MEMORY?

The memory is the human interference ability to encode, stock, and hold onto information or experiences in the brain to recall at a later point in time. Memory can use past experiences, previously learned information, to affect or alter our current behavior. As a significant element, in the process known as learning, memory deals with the total amount of everything that we have remembered and allows us to learn from our prior experiences and events. Overall, the memory is not only recalling the past, but also the interference ability to remembering experiences and facts we have previously learned. This makes it important for people or students pursuing ambitious careers like lawyers, accountants, doctors, businessman, politician, etc. think of our memory as our archive for facts and ideas we have learned, sorted, and retained from our everyday activities and experiences.

Memory is, by all means, most often used when we study. Studying alone carries two parts, which is learning and remembering. Learning refers to recognizing facts and ideas and understand their origins. Remembering what you've learned is the ability to place those facts and ideas into a mental storehouse of your brain to recall at a later point in time. To triumph in your studies, tests, examinations and performance-evaluated tasks it is essential to be able to understand both learning and remembering.

THREE DIFFERENT KINDS OF MEMORY

There are three various kinds of memory, and our brain and body use these particular kinds of memory in a number of ways, but also conspicuously affects the others:

SENSORY MEMORY: The first form of memory is called the sensory memory. Sensory memory is known as the shortest form of memory that the human brain carries. As the name implies, sensory memory is memory linked with sensations. For instance, any of your five senses, whether a sight, a scent, or a sound. Sensory memory is handled by various areas around the brain, most often those parts of the brain that are responsible for the particular sensation. The occipital lobe, the portion of the brain responsible for vision, is also responsible for memory storage on the sights we see every day. The fundamental point about this kind of memory is that information is only temporarily stored in the sensory memory unless it is passed through the short-term memory. It is for this reason that sensations are unable to be recalled with any precise feeling. We can recall any accounts of pain, but we are incapable of actually remembering the exact feeling we experienced. Rather, we must explain how we are feeling with words like sharp, itchy, cramp, burning, or stinging. Even as we recall this information, the feelings of pain never return because those sensations were processed by the brain and then discarded. The experience may have left a lasting enough effect to have been passed on to a longer form of memory, but the sensations will never be revived.

To sum this up, the sensory memory is formed by the sensory impressions that you receive through the five senses, most prominent amidst which are the visual and auditory senses. A sensory memory lasts for just a few seconds and has an unlimited quantity. It works by retaining a replica of whatever is seen or heard that you can't consciously control consciously.

SHORT-TERM MEMORY: The next sort of memory is recognized as the short-term memory. Short-term memory is the middleman between the shortest state of memory and the longest state of memory. However, unlike sensory memory, short-term memory is filled with the brain, but only for a couple of minutes. Generally, the short-term memory centers can only retain data for a maximum of five minutes. On the whole, short-term memory preserves anywhere from thirty seconds to one minute.

For instance, imagine somebody giving you a phone number in person. Once they provide you with this number, you try to repeat it back to yourself once or twice and begin to dial this number. You just used your short-term memory. Now, after the phone call, can you still recall the phone number? Most likely not. This is because short-term memory isn't stored in your brain for very long. Much of the information we gather throughout the day isn't necessary to actually remember, and if we stored all the information we read or used throughout the day, our brains would overflow with useless information. For this reason, our brain works by allowing short-term memories to come and go, thus enabling us to employ information briefly, and then move on, without wasting brain space.

LONG TERM-MEMORY: If our brain removes all our short-term information, you must be wondering how information is ever drawn back up? How can we learn if we are always throwing away all the knowledge we face? The answer to this prevails in the third form of memory known as long-term memory. Long-term memory, as the name implies, the longest kind of memory that the human brain holds. Long-term memory is what enables us to remember our names, birthdays, important dates, passwords, and all the important things. It allows us to know when to wake up and go to work. It grants us to know what kind of information to pull up at any given time for use. Of course, there are instances in which our long-term memory fails, but we will discuss this and solutions later in this book.

Different from short-term memory, long-term memory stores information in the brain permanently. This is because the information contained within our long-term memory collects what's relevant to our everyday life. Or you can rehearse long enough to force your brain to remember it. Hence, to go from short-term memory to long-term memory, the information or events must be given strict attention to. This is the reason why we remember important events and information in our lives rather than trivialities. The only information that we take the time to give importance to is permanently retained. For example, the phone number, if you keep dialing the number over and over again, you will eventually remember it. Repetition of the information is one way in which the brain learns and stores information. You have to make an effort and focus on information for it to go from being a short-term memory to long-term memory.

Therefore, understanding how your memory works are crucial for improving it. When you understand how your memory works, how we use our memory, and how we store them, we are better able to improve them and use the techniques listed. It is important to remember, but, that despite the fact that there are three kinds of memory, each form of memory works in harmony. Sensory memory information is either experienced and forgotten shortly after, or it is passed on to the short-term memory. If this sensory information is important enough and focused on, the information will be passed on from the short-term memory to the long-term.

Sensory memory can also be skipped entirely, and short-term memory can take over. This is the case with things such as names, birthdays, and special dates. You will either use the information instantly and then discard it, or you will recapitulate the information, hence efficiently moving it from short-term memory to long-term memory.

Now that we got to know that three kinds of memory, the obvious question is simple: Which kind of memory do you need to improve? Most people would like to say they want a better long-term memory. However, while it is true that an enhanced long-term memory can help you remember important academic or professional information in such a way that it remains there for the rest of your life, is it really necessary to remember less relevant information from your everyday affairs? Do you really need to know the full names of people you will likely only see once in your life? Do you really need to learn the Pledge of Allegiance in French? Do you really need to know the counties in Arizona? No, of course not. While trying to remember useless information is worthless, you can use it for practice. However, you should keep in mind that your short-term memory is just as useful for purpose as your long-term memory. Therefore, the techniques in this book will both improve your short-term memory and long-term memory.

CHAPTER 2: WHY YOUR MEMORY IS IMPORTANT

Memory is something that we use at each moment of our day, even when it looks like we're not sincerely using it. For instance, at this very second, I am using my recollection of the keys on the computer keyboard to type words. My brain concentrates on the content, but at the same time, I can recall what keys to press to make texts appear on the computer monitor right in front of me. Noticeably, while I continue to type, I do not gawk at my keyboard and recall where the keys on the keyboard are consciously. This all correlates to my working memory. In this section, we will read about the two types of memory recollection and how you can use your memory to help yourself stay organized.

Memory presents a significant role in our lives. It allows us to remember skills and information that we've learned, or reclaim information that is stored deep in our long-term memory centers, or recall a previous instant that happened in the past. Memory also organizes information so that when we recover it, we can apply that information in the general meaning and use it in the current activity we are indulged in.

To the greatest extent, we use short-term memory to retain information that we've received very freshly. Long-term memory is used to retain information that we've kept ever since childhood to the present day. In neuroscience, there is some interesting research about the kinds of memory we have access to as well as how memory adds to the overall senses a person contains.

IMPLICIT MEMORY is when you memorize things without really pondering about it. You can also regard your implicit memory as your body memory. For instance, breathing is part of your implicit memory. You never need to learn how to breathe. You just breathe from the moment you were brought into this world. As you continue to age, the things you learned (such as preparing food, writing in a journal, pumping gas, riding a bike, driving a car, talking to strangers, etc.) has to turn out to be an implicit memory attribute. You tackle your implicit memory each time you engage in an activity that contains some form of organization. The reason a person can prepare a meal, write in a journal, or drive a car even if they haven't engaged it in years is that of implicit memory. Your body commemorates how you handle complex activities such as driving a car because those motor skills get stamped in the autonomic division of the brain.

EXPLICIT MEMORY is the second kind of memory. Explicit memory happens when you attempt and consciously recall specific information. We mobilize our explicit memory regularly at a conscious level. You use your explicit memory when you ponder about last year's Thanksgiving feast. You use your explicit memory when you rush around your home, looking for the last place you put your wallet. You use your explicit memory when you try to think of when and where you and your date were supposed to meet. In addition, explicit memory also helps you recall precise details. Explicit memory is also what you use when typing or writing words and solving math equations.

Think of your memory as your brain's archive. Your memory contains all the things you have learned and went through ever since childhood. You can store an astounding quantity of information and events in there. For instance, as a child, you learn about ten new words a day. You might just know 100,000 or even more about now. You can recollect any of these words and their meanings because it's filed in your memory – as with so many other things! Your brain is a factual collection of information, and thus it's vital that you seek the need to improve it for better cognitive functioning and an overall improvement in life.

CHAPTER 3: WHY YOU SHOULD IMPROVE YOUR MEMORY

Are you happy with the memory abilities you already possess right now? If you haven't already come to the resolution on why you should put your energy into increasing your memory, here are a few benefits that go with this. If your memory is weak and prompting problems either in your professional or in your personal life, you most likely take your memory ability for granted.

There are countless of benefits to having a better memory other than being able to recall names, where you placed your wallet or remembering your anniversary date. A good memory will thrive in all stages of your life. A good memory will help in getting promotions at work as you will be able to pay absolute focus to instructions and details or what needs to be accomplished on a project. If you are a public speaker, a motivational speaker, a teacher, or even a politician, a good memory will provide you with an advantage when delivering presentations. If you are a businessman, a real estate agent, or an entrepreneur, it will help you memorize clients, business partners, and coworker's names and faces. As for students, good memory can help you retain information, formulas, data, procedures, and many other things to better your performance in school. In relationships, a good memory will help you remember important events and dates concerning your partner.

With all these reasons, why shouldn't you learn these memory methods?

Many people view memory loss as a mere case of developing their concentration, observation skills, or switching some adapted behavior to remember what they have learned. As for older people, they might have some sort of aging or chemical explanation as to why their memory is failing, but more than likely, a mere modification in diet and lifestyle, also doing some brain exercise, will help to make meaningful changes in their memory recognition.

Memory improvement techniques are not solely for people suffering from short-term memory loss. Learning new memory methods can help restructure your life, organize your life, decrease your stress levels, and even better your financial situation. We all have areas in our life that need improvement, and a good memory can undoubtedly help us in our endeavors.

Things such as memory training programs are becoming extremely high demand because people are more informed of how much importance they bear. Also, with our frantically busy world overloaded with information, learning new methods to keep everything secured and saved in our brain is becoming more relevant. We have to find means to enhance our short-term memory and our long-term memory to make our life manageable. As we progress in age, it becomes more necessary to simplify our lives to remain focused and retain what we learn and absorb.

So, how can learning any of these memory methods help you?

A good memory will help you stay organized in your brain and your overall life.

A good memory will help you understand that a healthy brain derived from a healthy body. As well with, your physical and mental health will improve.

Your professional and social life will improve. For instance, you will be able to evoke names and faces. You will be able to recall answers to questions without scrambling your notes. And most importantly, a good memory encourages productivity.

You will reduce a large amount of stress in your life caused by loss of memory and organization and train of thought.

An excellent memory means you can seize concepts and implement them in other situations, advancing your cognitive function. Your memory will see the bigger picture between these concepts and create netlike connections, increasing your knowledge.

A good memory will improve your social life and conversational skills as you can uphold a conversation because of an increased recall of incidents or memorabilia you have seen on the news. You will become a more well-balanced person, able to hold a conversation with anyone.

The benefits of a good memory are limitless, and the bigger your memory, the better you are to seize moments and take advantage of them. You would be surprised at what you have harnessed and regret not taking action to increase your memory earlier.

CHAPTER 4: MEMORY MYTHS DEBUNKED

In this section, we will debunk some of the most common memory beliefs and debunked them.

MYTH: It is attainable to create eternal memories. It is a popular belief that we can cherish memories strong enough never to lose sight of them.

FACT: As it is possible to acquire information adequately to make it impossible to forget them in our life. Each long-term memory, depending on its intensity, has an envisioned lifespan. If the memory is strong, the expected lifespan may be longer than our very own life. But, if we happened to get an extra three-hundred year to live, no memory store in present life would remain safe without recurrence.

MYTH: We never forget. A number of accelerated-learning and memory improvement programs insists that we never misremember what we learn and that information only gets misplaced, and the solution to achieve good memory is to find out how to uncover it

FACT: All information is exposed to continuous decay. Even your name, birthday, and address is unprotected. This is a matter of probability. Powerful memories are unlikely to be forgotten. The possibility of misremembering your name is the chance of the president knocking at your door: possible, but don't expect it is happening today.

MYTH: Many people believe we were born with infinite memory.

FACT: Anyone with basic understanding of memory knows that this claim is false. However, this is just one popular belief that is discrepant with primary school science level. After all, some people still believe that the Earth is flat. We cannot even dream to memorize an entire Encyclopedia in a human lifespan. Memories are collected in a limited number of states of limited receptors in limited synapses in a limited volume of the human central nervous system. Unfortunately, even storing information into your long-term memory is tough. The average person finds it difficult to memorize over 300-thousands facts in their lifetime.

MYTH: Sleeping for a lengthy amount of time is good for your memory. Many people believe that sleep and learning make us healthier and smarter.

FACT: All we require for effective learning is a well-organized sleep schedule. There's a lot of people who can sleep in less than 5 hours and wake up refreshed. However, many geniuses and successful people sleep very little and take mini naps throughout their day. Then, there's plenty of people who must sleep 10 hours to be refreshed. Long sleep may even be connected to illnesses. This is why research suggests that those who sleep seven hours live longer than those who sleep ten hours. The best recipe for good sleep is to listen to your body. Fall asleep whenever you are tired and sleep until you are well energized.

MYTH: As you continue to age, you will lose your memory. Aging will affect all parts of your body and mind. Almost half of people over 80-year-olds displays signs of Alzheimer's disease. Hence, the belief that your memory will get weaken with old age.

FACT: It is a fact that we lose neurons with old age. It is a fact that the risk of Alzheimer's disease raises with age. However, a well-trained memory is strong and shows fewer function signs of aging than other organs. Furthermore, training increases the horizons of your knowledge, and self-contradictory, your mental abilities may develop well at a very old age.

MYTH: You can boost your learning with memory pills. Countless companies market various drugs and supplements with claims of improved memory.

FACT: There are no such things as efficient memory pills. Many drugs and supplements obliquely help your memory by simply making you healthier. A healthier body is a healthier brain, and a healthier brain is a healthier memory. Many drugs and pills can boost your learning process itself, but these should not be primary to your interests. Let's take for instance that you are about to run a marathon. Now, there are foods and drugs that can help you run and improve your stamina, but if you are a runner, no pill can make you finish a marathon.

CHAPTER 5: UNDERSTANDING MEMORY LOSS

Don't get me wrong, we all forget where we put our wallets, IDs, keys, phones, and other essentials. We all occasionally enter a room forgetting why we enter in the first place. We all forget where we parked our automobile every once in a while. It's human nature to forget things! However, never-ending lapse of memory could lead to a more serious problem. Losing memory for the short-term is a mutual and bothersome problem, and in this chapter, we will learn all about it.

UNDERSTANDING SHORT-TERM MEMORY LOSS. For you to understand short-term memory loss, we are going to go over short-term memory once more. Ultimately, your short-term memory is the undertaking of temporarily collecting small portions of information for you to use under a small fragment of time – typically around thirty seconds to one minute. Regard short-term memory (STM) as scrap paper for jotting down notes. Here are several instances where you mobilize your STM on a typical day:

To shortly recall a cell phone number until you saved it on your phone.

To shortly recall an appointment date until you mark it in a calendar.

To remember the feedback you wish to make when someone is finished speaking.

To let yourself know to change lanes to make this right turn.

To recall your username and password to sign into your email or Facebook account.

To let yourself know what temperature to set the oven to bake a cake.

These sorts of information temporarily take place until you make an effort to commemorate. This implies that your short-term memory is important and only stores the trivial things in your life – think of your short-term memory acting as a mental filter, where it chooses the essentials and nonessentials information to feed your brain. Of course, nobody needs to recall each precise detail of everything that has approached them. You don't need to remember every single text in a book. You don't need to remember each second of your day. If you make this of importance, where is the quality? You will only clog your brain making it difficult to tell what's important and what's unimportant.

SOURCES FOR SHORT-TERM AND LONG-TERM MEMORY LOSS. Here are some of the most well-known contributors to memory loss. Do your best to avoid as many of these causes to the best of your ability for further memory enhancement:

MEDICATIONS: Plenty of prescriptions and buyable without prescription medications and drugs can result in the loss of memory.

ADDICTION: If you are addicted to alcohol, smoking, tobacco, or drugs, it can promptly be a reason for a cloudy mind.

BEING DEPRIVED OF SLEEP: Both the value of your sleep and the hours you sleep is imperative for good memory. If you get insufficient hours of sleep or insomnia, it can intervene with your capability to retain information.

STRESS & STRAIN: If you are low-spirited, it can make you more prone to losing information and affecting memory quality. Both stress and nervousness can hinder your focus. If you feel agitated, and your brain is overwrought or inattentive, your memory can deteriorate. Stress exacted by severe mental or physical pain can correspondingly direct to a memory loss.

LACK IN NUTRIENTS: The right number of nutrients, along with proteins and fats, is essential to good brain function. When you lack in Vitamin b1 and b12, it can impact your brain performance.

LIGHT OR TRAUMATIC BRAIN INJURY: If you suffered from either a light or harsh brain injury, whether from falling or from a car crash, it can profoundly affect your memory.

STROKES: Strokes arises when the blood supply to the brain is interrupted either from a blockage of a blood vessel or outflow of a vessel hooked on the brain. Strokes often lead to short-term memory loss, even long-term memory loss, but it can recover gradually.

WHEN TO SEARCH FOR HELP? To evaluate the roots of your loss in memory, visit a doctor or neurologist. The doctor or neurologist will check your medical antiquity and conduct a physical checkup, including a neurologic exam, and ask inquiries to test your mental capabilities. Depending on the outcomes, additional evaluations might involve blood and urine testing, and image analyses of the brain. At times, other examinations will be conducted as well. Treatments will depend on what's contributing to your memory loss.

However, the following memory enhancement techniques and methods can reinforce and heal your brain from memory loss and can help you develop a strong, healthy, and better memory.

CHAPTER 6: EFFECTIVE MEMORY IMPROVEMENT TECHNIQUES

We can all be jealous of people with extraordinary good memory. We all came across people who can remember every light thing with little to no trouble, while everyone else hassles to recall the name of the person they were just acquainted with. But, you have the power to change this. Like any other muscle, we can teach our brains to retain more and learn anything quicker. You don't need to be gifted with a total recall memory to accomplish this too. Supposing you need to study for an examination, craving to master a second language, need to commemorate important dates, wish to refrain from memory loss, or merely want to remain mentally sharp, elaborating your memory is simpler than it seems.

The many techniques in this portion of the book can drastically improve your memory. These methods can help you retain facts correctly and to retain the composition of information. As with any other skill, the more you practice, the more you become better with them. With plenty of training and commitment, you will be able to develop a memory as solid as a stone. These methods can also benefit and improve other areas of your life as well. With all this said, let's get started!

PRACTICE POSITIVITY AND BECOME AN OPTIMIST

I think it's harmless to say that the majority of us are around negative friends, coworkers, and even family members who candidly admit that they have a terrible memory. We might even be the ones believing we have awful memory ourselves. One of the reasons why people have bad memories is because they hold this limited, negative, and contemptuous outlook towards ourselves.

Unfortunately, those who linger in negative judging their mental abilities will never make any progression in memory enhancement. Why? Because when holding deep and negative beliefs that their memories are terrible, they are arranging a self-fulfilling prophecy that proclaims their memory is awful and will always remain awful. This provision will make you more prone to be discouraged time and time again. Nevertheless, there are profound psychological reasons as to why having a bad demeanor is directly associated with poor memory. These explanations take into record the basic activity of the brain and memory in correlation with both positive and negative mental states and how we choose to respond to those frames of mind.

Almost everything that you do is not free from emotion. From the easy tasks of tying your shoes, drinking a glass of water, reading a book, doing your job, or watching some video on the Internet; there is always some sort of positive or negative happening before us. While many us can't even sit in silence without some predominant emotional attitude clouding up our minds. Whether you are finishing a project under a tight deadline or at a friend's birthday party, life is covered with moments emotional responses from us. These emotional responses influence the information that we store in our brains. As a general guideline, it has been found that positive reactions and our feelings towards our experiences, all have a direct connection to our memory.

The human brain is predisposed to pick up negative stereotypes, according to a study that presents signs as to how prejudice arises and flow through modern civilization. But, looking from a physiological or psychological perspective, the human brain was never predisposed of negativity. Negativity occurs in two different sorts: external and internal. External negativity, as the name implies, is negativity that comes from outside forces. This can be in the form of insults, jealousy, criticisms, unfortunate events, or other people's actions, for the most part, there's nothing we can do about this. On the other hand, interior negativity emerges from negative emotions which appear throughout everyday events. The human mind conducts more than fifty-thousand thoughts a day, and most of these are negative. When the mind is coerced with too much information, it is incapable to comprehend most of that negative information exceeding the verge of one's short-term memory. When you are habitually negative, this can lead to depression and depression can lead to memory loss.

As human beings, we can control how we respond to both external and internal negative occurrences. While we cannot always guide our emotions, we can control the way we respond to those emotions. A positive approach to both external and internal negativity has been proven to improve long-term memory recognition. When you are in a cheerful mood, your thoughts, experiences, and information that the mind conducts become perpetually easier to recall. Somehow, information conducted under a positive attitude sticks into long-term memory with fewer resistance. This is the reason on why positive life lessons caused from unfortunate and negative experiences are often best retained.

Thus, when people say that they have an awful memory, they are merely reinforcing the fact that they have a reluctant attitude to remember facts. Therefore, the next time you learn something, you are subconsciously instructing your brain to forget almost immediately. As it may be tough to change your mood, you do have the choice whether to react to it constructively. So, rather than telling yourself you have a bad memory, tell yourself that you have a great memory that is growing better each day. When you install a positive mood from the beginning, you will be establishing a solid framework for the memory techniques ahead.

POSITIVE AFFIRMATIONS FOR MEMORY ENHANCEMENT

Developing a fantastically great memory can boost all aspects of your life, from improving your grades and school performance, to start up your career, to be more popular with those around you. These positive affirmations for memory enhancement can without doubt relief a foggy head so you can retain information from the initial time you hear it and call it up hastily.

Repeating these affirmations on a routine will empower you to recall important dates, names, faces, and facts easily and impulsively. If you stand firm and use them each day, you will surely become more mentally sharp and retain far more than most people. Declare these affirmations aloud or mentally in tune throughout your day for the best of benefits:

I remember information very swiftly.

My memory is improving by a ton.

I am an arsenal of new information and new knowledge.

I have a remarkable memory.

I am honing my memory and mental performance.

I am developing a strong and powerful memory.

I am building up my memory.

My focus is as sharp as a razor.

My memory is perfect.

I accurately remember things in grave detail.

I am well-known for my astonishing memory

I have a comprehensive brain.

I can always recall others birthdates.

I can easily recall any people's names and faces from the initial time we met.

I have a dependable, unfailing memory.

I can undoubtedly concentrate on any task at hand.

Recalling information is a simple process for me.

Everyone is impressed by my fabulous memory.

Everyone relies on me to remember information and I never fail them.

My mind is clear and in tune.

HEALTHY EATING FOR A BETTER MEMORY

If you wish to enhance your memory retention and cognitive performance immensely, you need to pay careful attention to your diet. Why? Because the kind of foods that you habitually eat and cerebral activity are very closely related.

A healthy, balanced, and nutritious diet that is rich in vegetables and fresh fruits is the foundation for proper brain function, as well as overall health. The right amount of nutrition can increase the blood flow to the brain and can support the synapses to build tougher and more resilient connections.

Do take notice and make sure that you consume plenty of omega-3 fatty acids and Vitamin D. Omega-3 fatty acids are found to be very vital for brain memory and cognitive performance, as well as behavioral function. An abundant source to find omega-3 fatty acids includes fish, vegetable oils, nuts, leafy vegetables, canola oil, cod liver oil, flaxseed oil, mustard oil, soybean oil, and walnut oil.

It has also been confirmed that when your calcitriol receptor, otherwise known as the Vitamin D receptor is activated, this helps to increase synaptic nerve growth in the cortex, particularly in the brain's vitally important hippocampus and cerebellum. These areas are crucial in the planning and processing of raw information arriving in your brain, along with the creation of new memories.

When your body lacks Vitamin D, it can result in impoverished brain function. Therefore, keeping your Vitamin D levels appropriately high will help maintain a state of mental wellness, especially in older people. So, where can you get your regular Vitamin D? Well, there's a multitude of ways, from sunlight exposure, fatty fish and tuna, dairy products, Vitamin D supplements, egg yolks, orange juice, beef liver, cod liver oil, and even exposure to ultraviolet lights found in tanning beds and light bulbs.

While we may think, we're eating healthily; we must also keep in mind that the alternative to a healthy diet is intermittent fasting. Since the beginning of time, mankind has practiced fasting to unwind their bodies to follow their religious and spiritual beliefs and to replenish and cleanse our physical body. When you are eating, as usual, your body uses glucose as fuel for the brain. When you fast and consume no-energy foods, your body shifts from burning glucose to burning unhealthy fats into ketones for fuel to the brain. This process commences after two or three days for most people. When you jump into a four to five-day intermittent fasting diet, you can overcome your appetite, restart your body and reduce your calorie intake, which just so correlates to promoting brain neuron growth and enhanced brain function. All that is required is be watchful and not to overdo it by going to extreme measures.

You should also listen to your gut, which is highly regarded as your second brain. This is because gut bacteria transfers information to your brain along the vagus nerve, which is the tenth cranial nerve that is linked to the gastrointestinal tract. Studies have even shown that there is a close connection between the abnormal gut flora and atypical brain development.

In addition, just as your brain contains neurons, your gut contains neurons as well, which produced neurotransmitters such as serotonin, which is a chemical located in your brain and which influences your mood. To put into terms, the condition of your gut can straightforwardly influence your brain function, overall mood and behavior.

BEST FOODS TO ENHANCE YOUR MEMORY, FOCUS, AWARENESS, AND BEHAVIOR

Healthy eating can lessen your exposure to diseases and illnesses such as diabetes, heart disease, hypertension, strokes, some cancers, and even Alzheimer's Disease. Here is a definitive list of some of the best foods you should implement in your diet for a better memory, focus, awareness, and even behavior:

AVOCADOS: Avocados are an exceedingly healthy fruit that everybody can enjoy. While avocados often get sidestepped because of their high-fat capacity, it's vital to realize that avocados consist of monounsaturated fats, which can lessen your chances of heart disease, prevent diabetes, alleviate your blood sugar levels, and keep your skin vibrant.

Avocados consist of both Vitamin K (20 micrograms, per 100 grams) and folate (80 micrograms, per 100 grams), which can refrain blood vessel leakage and damage. It can also promote cognitive function, specifically in both memory and concentration. As well with this, avocados are abundant in Vitamin B and Vitamin C, which is not produced biologically, meaning you must consume them each day.

Additionally, avocados have high-levels of protein and strikingly low-levels of sugar than any other kind of fruit. Consider implementing fresh and ripe avocados for smoothies, desserts, salads, salad dressings, or alone as a healthy snack!

BEETS: Beets is an astonishing ground vegetable to include in your diet. Despite the fact that beets contain the highest sugar capacity than the majority of other vegetables, you can still enjoy beet roots a couple times a week to reap its powerful benefits.

Beet roots are highly nutritious, anti-inflammatory, and contains many antioxidants which can lessen the risk of cancers and other diseases. Beets can also clear your blood of harmful toxins. The nitrates found in beet roots can boost blow flow to the brain, improving mental performance and clarity.

Beets are high in Vitamin C, dietary fiber, and essential minerals such as manganese and potassium. Beets also consists of Vitamin B and folate, which can refrain the likelihood of congenital disabilities. Recent studies show that weekly consumption of beet juice could provide better blood flow to the brain among seniors. This can utterly avoid the peril of memory dementia and Alzheimer's disease.

As well with this, after lengthy and exhausting workout sessions, beets can provide you with a quick burst of energy and improve your stamina afterward. Consider implementing beets in your salads or serve as a side dish!

BLUEBERRIES: Blueberries are delicious, luscious, healthy, and nutritious fruit. Blueberries, often recognized as a superfood for its low-calorie content and an enormous list of benefits. Blueberries consist of large volumes of phenols, particularly Gallic acid, which provides immense health advantages. One study from Iran suggests that we can shield brains from dementia, decay, neurotoxins, and oxidative stress and fatigue from frequent consumption of blueberries. How wonderful is that!

Another study found that consuming more blueberries can decrease cognitive decay and increase memory retention and brain function. Researchers believed these results were because of the antioxidants found in blueberries that babysit the body from oxidative stress and decrease inflammation.

BONE BROTH: Bone broth is a therapeutic superfood that can improve your brain, body, digestion, and gut feeling. Bone broth is chock-full with wellness benefits, extending from boosts in immunity, overpowering food allergies, improving joint health, crushing leaky guts, improves hydrations, improves mood, strengthens the bones, and even promoting weight loss.

In addition, the glycine contains in bone broth can replenish your cells from harmful chemicals and toxins which can enhance brain and cognitive function. Try your best to drink at least eight-ounces of bone broth in the early mornings for the best of benefits.

CELERY: Celery is a vegetable that is extremely low in calories, which correlates to a mere 16 calories per cup (or 6 to 8 calories per medium stalk). Celery offers an abundance of benefits. The gains of celery start by providing an exceptional supply of antioxidants and valuable enzymes. Also, a brilliant basis for vitamins and minerals like Vitamin K, Vitamin C, Vitamin B6, potassium, and folate. Since celery stalks contain so few calories, you can practically eat them every moment of the day without a single shred of regret.

COCONUT OIL: Up to the present time, there have been over 1700+ studies proving coconut oil to be one of the healthiest foods on Earth! Coconut oil carries with a humongous list of benefits as there are countless uses for coconut oil. There's practically nothing that coconut cannot assist you with.

Coconut oil has been a proven natural treatment for Alzheimer's Disease. The consumption of coconut oil by the liver produces ketone that is voluntarily available to the brain for natural energy. These ketones then provide energy to the brain without the demand of insulin to transform glucose into energy.

Studies show that the brain produces its own insulin to transform glucose and power brain cells. For those with Alzheimer's loses the capability to generate its own insulin. The ketones from coconut oil could serve as an excellent source of energy to help repair brain function.

And when it comes to your brain, it's covered by helpful benefits too. Coconut oil works as a natural anti-inflammatory, overwhelming cells accountable for inflammation and arthritis. It can also help with memory loss as you grow in age and extinguish harmful bacteria that loiter in your gut.

DARK CHOCOLATE: Dark chocolate is delicious, yummy, and beneficial as well! Dark chocolate increases moods, look after the brain from injury, improves memory and focus, decreases stress, and much more!

Dark chocolate is stocked of flavonols, which have antioxidant and anti-inflammatory properties. Dark chocolate also helps lower blood pressure and strengthen blood flow for the brain and for the heart. However, this doesn't mean you should eat five bars of Hershey's Chocolate every day. Most of the chocolate you find in grocery stores carry insufficient benefits and can actually be harmful to your brain. The guideline to follow when eating chocolate is the darker the chocolate, the healthier it is.

LEAFY GREENS AND CRUCIFEROUS VEGETABLES: Obviously, any vegetables can be immeasurably beneficial for your brain, memory retention, and cognitive function, hence, it is essential to implement lots and lots of vegetables in your diet.

Researchers found improvement in cognitive activity in people who devour larger numbers of green leafy vegetables. Researchers found that people who eat one to two servings per day had the cognitive capability of someone eleven years younger than those who consume none.

Green and leafy vegetables are also packed with Vitamins A and Vitamins K which can reduce inflammation and maintain strong bones. Such green and leafy vegetables include kale, spinach, swiss chard, arugula, spinach, bok choy, cabbage, asparagus, green beans, collards, etc.

In addition to green leafy vegetables, other excellent supplies for Vitamin K, lutein, and folate include brightly colored vegetables and fruits which include corn, oranges, bell peppers, tomatoes, carrots, grapes, pineapples, potatoes, onions, and berries.

REGULAR PHYSICAL EXERCISE FOR A BETTER MEMORY

Regular physical exercise is proven to become a powerful memory enhancer. As there are countless of other reasons to become physically fit: an improvement in memory and cognitive ability is one of them. During workout sessions and exercising, nerve cells dispense proteins recognized as neurotrophic factors One, specifically, recognized as brain-derived neurotrophic (or BDNF for short) release many different preservatives that increase overall neural wellness and immediately benefit the cognitive functions, including learning and memory retention.

Obviously, there are so many reasons why you should exercise! Apart from greater memory retention and cognitive abilities Daily exercising can lower the perils of heart disease, diabetes, stroke, flue, cancers, and other illnesses. Among other things shedding off fat and looking physically better! More importantly, one of the derivative gains of routinely workout sessions is that it clearly aids the brain to reduce brain fog that derives in all of us with the relentless stream of time.

The finest type of exercise for an improvement in memory is daily aerobic exercise. Apart from getting your heart and sweat glands thrusting, aerobics have been scientifically proved to expand the volume of the hippocampus, which is the area of the brain that is intimately linked with verbal memory and comprehension.

By opposition, resistance training, weight lifting, and muscle toning exercises have been shown not to have the equal beneficial effects as aerobics. Aerobic exercises (among them include running, biking, swimming, and gymnastics) supports memory retention and brain function, both directly indirectly.

Exercise provides **DIRECT** help by decreasing insulin struggle, lessening inflammation, and by inciting the discharge of growth elements. The latter are specific brain chemicals which influence brain cell health, cell development, and the operative of blood vessels to these cells.

Exercise provides **INDIRECT** assistance by improving our behavior, our mood, our quality of sleep and by reducing worry and stress. If you have trouble in these four areas, it can drastically influence your memory, mind, and physical health.

Studies show that the medial temporal cortex and the prefrontal cortex, which are the scopes of the brain monitoring the roles of understanding and memory have far better quantity among people who work out than those who don't. Even daily exercise of modest ferocity over the duration of half a year has been proven to result in a substantial enhancement in the volume of several crucial brain regions. However, you may be asking yourself, how much exercise do I need?

Research implies that a sixty-minute walk, two times a week is a great starting point as this equates to 120 minutes of moderately intensive exercise per week. This routine can then be drawn-out to doing thirty minutes of moderate physical exercise for four days, or better yet, each day of the week. This might come off as overwhelming though. Hence, you can begin gently and build your routine gradually until you mark the distinction in your cognitive abilities and clarity of mind.

But remember, you're not trying to become a professional athlete (unless you want to). You are simply exercising your body so that your mind can begin operating at its full potential.

Organize a regular habit and routine of exercising as well, because, in this manner, the likelihood to quit diminishes due to a healthy lifestyle. Whatever the case, don't make any sort of excuse. Make sure that daily aerobic exercise becomes an elemental role of your style of life. You will mark the difference in your clarity of thinking and your skills in receiving and incorporating raw information.

BRAIN-TRAINING ACTIVITIES FOR A BETTER MEMORY

Your brain can store up to 2.5 petabytes of information, which equates to three million hours of video watching! Storing in information into your natural storage is one thing, being able to retrieve that knowledge is different. However, playing brain and memory games are known to develop mental dexterity and promote better memory retrieval.

CROSSWORDS, for instance, is a marvelous way to enhance cognitive functioning and delay the arrival of dementia. So, if you are bored out of your mind or out on lunch, do a crossword to get your brain neurons moving. However, you shouldn't do them for hours.

Research suggests that those who are proficient at crossword puzzles reach a short of memory level where they're not actually increasing their memory retention at all because they simply become skilled at a learned ability.

JIGSAW PUZZLES are another fabulous way to flex your short-term memory as the brain must process a whole sequence of shapes and color to bring together an orderly visual picture. The larger the jigsaw puzzle is, the more your brain can be put into motion. Your brain also takes in dopamine, which is a neural chemical which aids concentration after completing the puzzle.

CHESS may serve as the memory game of highest quality since a good player must analyze and remember so many potential chess moves in advance. It challenges your mind to think three steps or even a hundred steps ahead. Chess grandmasters are memory athletes who hold entire chess strategies to their long-term memory. And therefore, making the opening plot of their game acts of memory far more than intelligence. Try playing a game of chess once a week with someone or similar cleverness and notice your memory progress every week. If you don't have a real chess board, don't worry. There are many apps where you can play chess on your phones and with bots and without having to clean up afterward.

THE SUITCASE GAME is another great game that can aid your memory. This game does require more than two people at least. To play, the first person begins by starting an item that he plans to pack in a make-believe suitcase, trailed by the next thing by a different person, and so on and so on. At some point in time, you will be forced to recall a very extended list of the things you filled in your suitcase which will really help expand your memory. The first person to forget a certain thing in the precise order loses. The Suitcase Game is an excellent brain game that you can play in your study groups or long rides on a bus.

THE TRAY GAME is another simple and easy game. You do need another person. In this game, you will spread a bunch of small items onto a serving tray and take a brief peek at the tray before covering it with a cloth. Then, you will try to remember all the things you saw on the tray. It may sound simplistic, but it's one of the best games for training object-recall, an important component of short-term memory.

SUDOKU is a great and more of a cerebral challenge for memory enhancement. In this game, you will need to retain a sequence of numbers in your head while mentally preparing where you will put them in a nine-space grid. This game you access your working memory intensively. But as with crossword puzzles, limit your intake before your brain grown used to organizing all the numbers. If it begins to get easier, it's time to move on and find something new.

CHANGING HANDS, this easy and practical brain exercise can be an excellent workout and may even turn you into an ambidexter. If you are dominantly left-handed, use your right hand to perform easy tasks such as brushing your teeth, cooking, eating, scrolling through your own, etc. If you are dominantly right-handed, use your left hand to grab things, open doors, and even writing. can be tricky at first but switching up your dominant hand can surely increase brain activity.

BRAIN YOGA, brain yoga is an incredibly inexpensive and fantastic brain game that can help both your memory function and the gray matter of your brain. To perform brain yoga, use your left hand and form a fist. Then, stretch your thumb far out. Do the same thing with your right hand, but this time, only stretch your pinky. Now change them at the corresponding time, so this time around it's the left pinky stretching and right thumb stretching. Tough, isn't it? The directions associated will encourage your neural connections, thus your memory.

VIRTUAL BRAIN TRAINING GAMES can provide an easily accessible and effective training for your memory, focus, and brain. There's countless of free apps you can download on your mobile device that can encourage an improvement in memory. Here is a couple of games that you should check out:

- Lumosity
- Dakim
- Eidetic
- Clevermind

- Brain Trainer

- Brain Metrix

- Fit Brains Trainer

- Cognifit Brain Fitness

- And so much more!

OBSERVER TEST is a fun little exercise that can put your observation skill and focus to the test. Using the picture below you must try to locate the numbers sequentially from one to ninety and you can not mark the figures you found. Give it a go!

If you sequentially locate all ninety numbers in:

- 5 to 10 minutes, then you have first-rate observation and memory skills

- 10 to 15 minutes, then you have decent observation and memory skills

- 15 to 20 minutes, then you have average observation and memory skills

- 20 to 25 minutes, then you have satisfactory observation and memory skills

- 30+ or gave up, then you have below average observation and memory skills

REFINING YOUR MEMORY WITH NIGHT'S SLEEP

There's no science behind it, but we all perform to the best of our abilities after a good night's sleep. A vibrant, clear, and aware mind allows us to concentrate, comprehend, learn, and recall information with ease. Furthermore, when we are tired and drowsy, you are prone to make more blunders and become unproductive in your professional and non-professional duties.

Healthy sleep patterns place you in the appropriate mental state to store fresh information as you go throughout your day to day living. Aside from that, we all need the right hours of sleep for progression and to store information in our long-term memory. Sleep, in fact, activates changes in the brain that strengthen memories – firming up networks between neurons and shifting information from one section to another.

Harvard University Research studied on the memory and suggested that the hours and quality of sleep contributes profoundly to both learning and memory. Studies suggest that people are 33% more expected to understand connections and relations between slightly related ideas after having a good night's sleep. Where sleep-deprived people were helpless to concentrate their attention successfully and therefore cannot acquire raw and fresh information effectively. Sleep also has a vital role in the consolidation of memory, which is essential for long-term memory.

However, the definite reason for this is still research. The process of brain growth, known as neuroplasticity, happens when neurons are excited by experiences, events, or information taken from your surroundings. Sleep and sleep loss were believed to accustom certain DNA segments which might be crucial for synaptic plasticity. Data acquisitions and data consolidations are closely linked together, even if the latter is achieved through diligence. Memory formation is achieved during periods of sleep and dreaming. It is during this time where activity is cut short that the brain strengthens the neural networks which create our memories.

Through the perspectives of memory researchers, the different stages of sleep are involved in the strengthening of memories, and when a person is sleep-deprived, their memory is unfavorably insufficient. The brain undergoes different phases of sleep at night. The deepest phase of sleep is known as slow-wave sleep and this period is vital in the fortification of memories. The section of the brain called the hippocampus is also important in the formation of memories, especially episodic memories, which connect the different aspects of memory together. Research shows the neurons in the hippocampus were triggered when learning a new course through chaos became active during slow-wave sleep. The restoration of these neurons to strengthen the new neural links in the brain.

Recent research indicates that one of the best ways to improve your memory is to take a light break when you are learning something new. This is because when you take a break, it reinforces the trace of the information we have just enforced to memory, and this has the power of making your memory easier to retrieve information in good time. Research from Oxford University proven this claim as they conducted an experiment between two groups of people ranging in their sixties to eighties years of age. Both groups were given information in the form of a story. However, one group was allowed a short period of wakeful rest after hearing the story; the second group was made to play a simple game which employed their mind. Sometime later all the participants were given a spot test to determine their powers of remembrance. Those who had sat and relaxed their minds for only ten minutes had a much higher ability to recall than those whose minds have been fatigued by the game.

Eventually, all the participants were given a spot test to determine their powers of remembrance. Those who had rested their minds for just ten minutes had a much higher ability to recall than those whose minds have been fatigued by the game.

The associations of this experiment are that whether you are trying to recall information for an examination, or pitch a business strategy to a potential client, or even pass a phone message to someone, if you rest briefly while after having committed the information to mind it may make all the difference between smoothly recalling their information at a later point in time against shaking your brain to try and summon it forth. Today, however, we are barraged with an infinite stream of information every second of the day. Nonetheless, even in our informational charged world we still owe it to ourselves to lay down on our bed and take a nap. Because a short period of wakeful rest after acquiring new and fresh information can mean all the difference in remembering information for later recall, even if we are not intentionally rehearsing the details of what we've just learned.

Chronic fatigue might be one of the worst things for your memory. Why? Because when you are frequently sleep deprived, your focus, concentration, comprehension, and attention will be unsteady to store new information successfully. Moreover, the failure to gain sufficient hours of sleep can cause our brain's neurons to become incapable of organizing what little information we can absorb. The total amount of this process is that in the absence of the ability to obtain, assemble, and remember information properly we become unable to make sound decisions and our overall judgment becomes confronted. When you are chronically fatigued, your brain neuron's refuse to activate precisely and your physical body and its organs are not functioning right, as they should be taking in the appropriate amount of rest. A poor mood may be the direct correlation and has fundamental implications for both learning and memory.

The bottom line is to really supercharge your memory get adequate sleep each night and take micronaps throughout your day. As synaptic connections are reinforced while you sleep, just think of it as using good rest and power naps to grow more retaining skills.

REDUCING OR ELIMINATING STRESS TO ENHANCE MEMORY

One of the most elemental methods to help enhance your memory is to reduce or eliminate the levels of stress amongst your life. As a matter of fact, stress-reduction carries a multitude of benefits for your life and is vital for maximum brain functioning. When you feel stressed, you use up too much mental energy by frustration, and this means that you end up with less accessible mental energy to store information in your long-term memory centers for you to recall later. Moreover, when you feel nervous, your muscles will tense up, causing them to use more oxygen than normal. As a result of you are redirecting more oxygen to the body and muscles, this implies that your brain receives less oxygen than it needs to perform its functions well.

Stress also produces a hormone in your body known as cortisol. Related to the popular fight-or-flight response, cortisol is viable for short periods, but when your body creates it for a number periods of time, cortisol becomes very unhealthy. This is because cortisol is completely harmful to your brain's neurons. As a matter of fact, chronic and protracted periods of stress can actually multiply your chance of being diagnosed with Alzheimer's disease. Recent research shows that particular kinds of stress-reducing activities can prevent this toxic cortisol reaction and benefit maximum functioning of the brain and memory. For that reason, effective stress management strategies are essential for good brain performance. You can practice this in a couple of ways: by collecting your thoughts, quieting your mind, and relaxing.

Sometimes the imperativeness to recall all the diminutive information of day to day living can be highly stressful. If you collect your thoughts, you can alleviate stress and aid your memory to perform its task better. This could be something as simple as writing your tasks in a calendar or organizer, anything which will help you collect your thoughts together in a single place the techniques for recalling these lists of tasks from memory will follow later, don't worry. But for the moment concentrate on trying to reduce stress by making your life easier.

Another thing you can do to reduce stress is to ease your mind. Buddhists have practiced this method for thousands and thousands of years, and we've only realized the benefits of an enlightened mind since the last hundred years when eastern meditation methods started coming to Europe from the Orient. We will engage in mediation in more detail in the following section, but at the moment, do your best to reduce the constant babbling that goes on endlessly inside your head.

Yoga practitioners call this chatter the monkey mind and it can be a tremendous source of worry and stress having to listen to your thoughts charging along like uncontrolled and stampeding horses. When you ease your own mind, you will observe that you are able to listen to others more effectively, and efficient listening is the foundation for memory recall.

Lastly, you should employ relaxation techniques. Always try to relax your mind. When your mind and body reach a relaxed physical and mental state, you will be less mentally agitated, and it becomes easier to absorb, retain, and then recall information. Most often we give ourselves unnecessary stress by being worried about not being able to remember something. It is sort of like being worried about being worried, a completely unproductive waste of your precious mental energy. Relaxation is admittedly hard in today's frantic 24/7 world, especially if you live in the big city or have a demanding profession. We also sometimes feel guilty about indulging in relaxing pursuits, thinking that we should be more productive in order to justify our existence. We need to learn to let these acquired attitudes go and accept that we need and deserve moments of relaxation.

One condition which has been shown to be advantageous for brain health is the gentle Chinese martial art of Tai Chi. Tai Chi consists of an explicit sequence of graceful, flowing bodily postures and associated movements. An eight-month study conducted by the University of South Florida found that seniors who engaged in Tai Chi just three times a week underwent a significant improvement in brain volume and achieved higher marks in memory tests and cognitive abilities. Tai Chi can also contribute to the major improvements in strength, flexibility, agility, posture, and balance. Tai Chi can revamp your mind to become more relaxed and less agitated. Sooner or later, the new patterns of calmness and quietness which you have acquired will remain as habitual traits, and consequently, your ability to absorb and recall will benefit.

The next time you choose to remember where you left something, your car keys or your wallet, stress will automatically block your memory recall. Breathe deeply and exhale slowly. In a calm manner, reconstruct all the things you have done up until that point and more often than not the resting place of your missing items will turn out instinctively!

HOW MEDITATION EXPANDS YOUR MEMORY RETENTION

As outlandish as it sounds, meditation and memory are indistinguishable connected. Scientific research has proven that when a person meditates, they are literally shifting their physical structure of the brain in astonishing and beneficial ways which include data acquisition and memory retention.

A study was conducted by Dr. Sara Lazar at the Psychiatry Department of the Massachusetts General Hospital in Boston which showed that regular mindfulness meditation actually causes the brain's cerebral cortex to thicken.

Recent studies suggest that regular mindfulness meditation literally affects the brain's cerebral cortex to stiffen. The study found that the stiffening of the brain's cerebral cortex is provoked by an increase in the size of blood vessels and the general blood flow in the cerebral region. This was specifically so in the brain's outer cortex, which is solely responsible for the higher mental functions like concentration, comprehension, and memory. Astonishing enough, this was all pushed forward by just meditation!

Meditation seemingly helps cerebral functioning across a number of various levels along these lines. Before anything else, it aids the mind gaining strength by implanting in us high levels of stillness, concentration, and focus. When you meditate, you are strengthening your mind and working that mental muscle, prolonging the life of the brain, preventing the onset of early memory loss. Along with, meditation has been made known to delay the aging process by reducing your stress levels, which remains a significant factor in fast-tracked aging and memory loss. Many doctors, neurologists, and researchers have even gone as far to describe regular meditation as the unspeakable health-giving fountain for both the body and mind.

Mediation professedly touches into your vacant, subconscious memory centers, assisting you to recall information and events in your life which will never be lost, you can only lose the ability to access them again. Meditation is one of the key instruments for accessing forgotten memories in a healthy and natural manner and remains one of the most effective ways to mobilize the power of the subconscious mind. This is because meditation activates those specific centers of the brain that are linked with long-term memory, which is the hippocampus and frontal brain lobe, both of which are said by researchers in this field to light up during meditation experiments.

Another significant analysis was directed from the University California in which forty-eight undergraduates took either a mindfulness class or a nutrition class. The mindfulness class, which was given by meditation professionals, emphasized the physical posture and mental strategies of focused-attention meditation. Thereupon, both groups of students took the standardized Graduate Record Examinations (GRE for short) tests for their grade school applications. The result of the study found that test scores among the group which had to participate in the meditation classes improved versus those in nutrition classes. Their average GRE scores raised from 460 to 520 in only a half-month. This suggests that taking the time to reflect your thoughts, your breathing, your body, your mind, your posture, and your soul can expressively improve your general cognitive functioning and performance.

But what kind of meditation method should you proceed in? Well, there are several ones to select from. The well-known Transcendental Meditation method, or TM for short, was familiarized by the West and promoted by the Beatles in the early 1960s. This method does require extensive training and devotion although it can require as little as twenty minutes practice a day.

The other kind of meditation is Mindfulness Meditation, which is extremely powerful. Mindfulness Meditation is a Buddhist-based breathing method which has been extensively studied and found to be highly beneficial to one's overall health. Studies on mindfulness-based stress reduction (or MBSR) showed that it was helpful in reducing chronic pain, chronic fatigue, diminishing anxiety, and in healing all kinds of illnesses. In MBSR, you are must practice at least 30 minutes per session and empty your mind of thoughts and solely focus on your breathing.

To begin meditating, just follow these simple steps:

First off, find a comfortable place to sit. Make sure it's a quiet and suitable spot which is free of any sort of distractions.

Then, close your eyes and start taking deep breaths through your nose. Bring all your focus to and awareness to each single breath you take. Pay close attention to the sound of your breath, how it feels entering your nostrils and into the lungs. Each time something comes to disrupt your focus, bring your attention back to your breathing. Never try to force away any thoughts which enter your mind, just accept them and go back to focusing on your breath! Do this each day and feel your memory taking strength over time while at the same time improving your memory.

Don't be discouraged if you find that you have many thoughts and feelings trying to distract you. This is very common for beginners, and you will gradually grow past these distractions through dedicated practice. Try to meditate longer and longer to help you feel more aligned with yourself Meditation doesn't always have to be performed by focusing on your breathing patterns. If you can align your awareness to a single moment, a single thing, or a single task and refocus when disturbed, you are meditating. For instance, if you are sitting outside listening to nature with soothing music playing in the background, that can be a focal point for meditating.

Meditation and stress reduction are both highly effective methods to enhance your memory. Learning both of these methods will dramatically improve your memory, your concentration, and emotional condition.

HOW YOUR LEARNING ENVIRONMENT CAN AFFECT YOUR MEMORY

Your study environment can have a straight influence on your learning and memory abilities. At first, this may seem apparent. Learning in a silent room is, of course, going to be much easier and effective than learning in a noisy cafeteria. However, there is deeper scientific evidence for this claim. Research from the Iowa State University experimented on university students who read an article in a noisy and silent environment. The research found that your environmental settings seemed to be more critical for recognition and recall of raw information than for the recognition of already accustomed information. Moreover, when you are doing essays which require for you to draw facts from memory, there is a direct correlation between environmental context and memory, where memory traces can be used to enhance retrieval of information. Fascinating enough, the same researchers found that excessive noise in the background did not seem to influence memory recall or studying adversely, but due of being present, it was nonetheless recommended that students are better off studying without any background noise.

So much for studying while watching your favorite show in the foreground. But how about we question the nature of your learning environment. Whether your atmosphere is enriched or impoverished from a cognitive viewpoint. Research from Tufts University proven that not only does an animal nurtured environment have a profound effect on its ability to learn and remember, but also that these effects can be congenital. Through an experiment performed on mice, researchers found that we are not a simple collection of our genes. Our actions can make a vast difference. Specifically, they learned that enriched environments encourage the synaptic strengthening of a sort which supports both information engagement and memory recollection. The researchers put some mice into an enriched environment full of toys and other mice. They also put some mice into an impoverished environment without any toys. Their findings found that the hippocampus of the brain is distinctly superior to the mice which had been nurtured in enriched environments.

So, how can you enrich your own learning environment? Well, there are many ways for you to do this. One simple way is to have a bookshelf covered with books inside your office or studying area. The trend these days towards decluttering and minimalist environments come with loads of benefits. But the mere fact that some of the greatest philosophers, greatest thinkers, greatest writers, throughout history added their innovative research and studies into a final coated book. When you surround yourself by the greatest minds of history through the form of books, it can serve as a constant reminder of all the great intellects which have lived on before us.

Another thing that you can do is immerse in great music. Studies have found that children and adults who listen to Mozart music for just twenty minutes a day performed better overall on their tasks. This even has a name relating to this, known as the Mozart Effect, and it can make anyone more intelligent.

Try to change up your environments as well. Go for long walks, go to the beach, visit a park, visit a museum, set time for fun! Other motivating things you can do consists of going to art museums, going to the orchestra, admiring architecture, going to church or temples. When you actively go out to fresh new locations, you are given in to your cognitive apparatus to a much greater degree of sensory stimuli, which is more enriching than only lingering in one place the entire time. So many people attempt to study their learning material in a noisy and crowded area. Study somewhere quiet and enriching for you to get the most out of memory retention and effective learning.

HOW MULTITASKING INFLUENCE YOUR MEMORY RETENTION – AND HOW TO AVOID IT

Whether you are scrolling mindlessly through your Facebook feed while watching the Game of Thrones premiere, seeking to while at the same time watching the morning news, or perhaps buying stuff on Amazon while getting started on dinner. Multitasking can take a huge toll on your brain and memory retention. Studies have proven that shifting your concentration between one task to another can make you more at risk to retain less information. Multitasking can also release harmful hormones that can affect your train of thought, and might even lower your IQ levels. According to research conducted by the University of Copenhagen, productivity, focus, and memory retention decreases in people who use their technological devices and gadgets while at the same time doing something else.

When you begin to concentrate on one thing at a time, your brain receives information and transfers it to your hippocampus, where the information is classified for smooth memory in the time to come. When you divert your thought process from task to task, the information simply cannot be refined fast enough.

Instead, information goes to your striatum, another region of your brain which is in charge for forecasting actions and motivations rather than storing information. Meaning, when it comes to multitasking, you are actually losing information rather than retaining it.

On top of that, research also suggests that when you send constantly send information to the striatum, you are setting up a routine and rewiring your brain to place fresh information in the incorrect places. This can create long-term memory problems. Studies also have proven that multitasking can scale down the gray matter in your brain, which influences everything from muscle control, self-control, memory retention, sensory perception (such as hearing, seeing, etc.) decision making, speech, and emotions.

Another study published in the Proceedings of the National Academy of Sciences suggests that multitasking can take a huge toll on the functional memory in older people. With all this research, the harmful actions of multitasking can split our attention, divide our concentration and throttle our cognitive abilities and memory retention. These recent studies can be shocking to many taking in the fact that we are living in an insanely busy and frantic world Now, we may all believe that we're productive and efficient by doing more things at once, going from social media to social media, device to device, task to task, however, we are only more ineffective and fruitless as before.

For instance, how often do you find yourself going to the grocery store to pick up milk, only to return home with a shopping bag filled with groceries with everything except milk? How annoying could that be! It's not because we "forgot" it, but there's a scientific explanation for this. It is because of the ability to change back to the original task at hand, once having been distracted by something else. This is far difficult for our mental structures to deal with on its own.

Whenever you are multitasking, you are adjusting your focus of your attention back and forth, from one thing to another. The tasks at hand you are trying to finish is not receiving the required mental focus or attention to complete it successfully. Studies have proven that the human brain needs at least eight seconds to process any piece of information extensively. When you multitask, you are short-changing that mission critical memory process and hence, not retaining anything at all.

The risk of multitasking comes at a great price. Poor-quality work and poor performance may risk the future of your career and ruin opportunities. The consequences for multitasking can be even worse as throwing and catching lots of different tasks or information can be extremely stressful. And stress can impact both your memory function and your health. One example or reckless multitasking is when someone is trying to take care of a toddler while at the same time, cooking, vacuuming and talking with a friend over the phone. It's too much for your brain to process at the time! You must be able to prioritize the tasks and concentrate fully on one task at a time. Many people so adamantly believe that productivity depends on doing many different things at once. However, productivity isn't about the quantity of your work, but the quality. It's not about working hard; it's about working smarter.

Unless you are a wedding planner where you need to keep your eye on every small thing, no task requires you to multitask, even though you may convince yourself into thinking that it does. The brain is not compatible for handling a frenzy of a variety of tasks. If you don't believe me, try for yourself. Grab a book and try to read it while at the same time preparing dinner or talking to someone over the phone. It will end up a mess. But, why do so many people believe that we can multitask effectively? There's no reason at all. It's only because we have believed a misleading belief that we have extraordinary superhuman abilities when in truth, we don't.

To a greater extent, your brain deals with the frenzy of tasks created by multitasking by pumping out adrenaline and other damaging hormones which can drive you insane. These chemicals and hormones might offer a quick burst of energy, but a consistent flow of stress-related hormones can strain your body and disrupt your overall health. Certainly, work related and non-work-related stress can lead to chronic health issues, such as back pain, heart disease, illnesses, and depression.

When it comes to affecting your memory retention; multitasking can dramatically impact your short-term memory for the worse. The reason for this is because when you are multitasking, you will have less attention available to save memories and information. For example, one person simply cannot talk to a client or business partner over the phone while reading emails. They will simply not have the attention to either remember parts of the conversation or remember important information in the emails. Additionally, short-term memory loss can cause your system to flood with adrenaline and other hormones which have been released due to the efforts of dealing with many tasks at once. You can even cause permanent impairment to the specific kinds of brain cells and neurons which store your memories. Eventually, after years and years with constant multitasking and no attempt on ridding of it, it can affect your ability to solely focus on one task at a time out of habit.

The bottom line is when you are working on something that needs your undivided attention and memory retention, eliminate all sorts of distractions and don't be tempted to work on things. Breathe deeply and think about the thing you need to focus right in front of you. Don't be persuaded into the misbelief that you can memorize your psychology notes while watching your favorite television show. Don't think that you can read a book while preparing dinner. You can always put things aside and do the more urgent things first. If you want to get more done in little time possible, stop multitasking. It will place you in a better position for the other memory techniques throughout the book.

MASTER NEW ACTIVITIES TO IMPROVE YOUR MEMORY

When you keep busy in strong-willed and worthwhile activities, this triggers the neurological system. The key element crucial for enhancing your brain function and memory retention is the motivation behind your tasks. Particularly, the task must carry some meaning to you or must have caught your interest. The task should be something that you actually look forward and excited to do, such as a chosen hobby. For instance, people will retain the details of an interesting novel than retaining lessons from a boring lecture. Whatever the case, it must captivate your attention.

Such hobbies require a substantial mental investment in the memory areas of the brain's cortex. Learning how to play a musical instrument, for example, requires both mental and muscle memory. Memorizing and rehearsing poetry lines, lyrics to a song, lines from a script is another way to enhance your memory in a fun and determined fashion. Such hobbies require all your focus and dedication for you to enjoy them.

Researchers from the University of Texas investigated this claim by aimlessly appointing 200 people to engross in various activities. Some people learned digital photography, photoshop, cooking, knitting, bowling, chess, gardening, woodworking, and other activities. These individuals dedicated up to 15 hours a week for a period of 3 months practicing and developing these new skills. Three months later, they were given a memory test. They were also compared with a group who engaged in unusual activities like watching television, watching movies and internet surfing. The research indicated that not all activities are designed equally and not only those test subjects who learned a new skill experienced significant gains. The greatest improvement was seen in people who learned digital photography and Photoshop because they deemed the most challenging. The greatest improvement was seen in those people who learned digital photography and Photoshop because they were the most difficult.

So, what's the connection between mastering new skills and memory improvement? It's because mastering new skills strengthens the connections between different scopes of your brain. While playing brain games can help enhance your short-term memory, engaging in more thought-provoking pursuits strengthens your entire neurological system in the brain. The heightened relatedness is the key to enhanced memory retention. However, it must be emphasized that while the new hobby or skill can be practically anything of a challenge, it must be something you really enjoy and reap happiness from. One of the best hobbies that everybody enjoys and loves to do is reading. Reading also inspires you to access new concepts and ideas which force your mind to flex and take on these new ideas. Reading is also an exceptional mental workout for the mind and its memory centers.

Some human beings have naturally active minds which are always striving to stretch their professional and personal knowledge. You can always expand your intelligence through adventure, travel, experience, the physical senses, or through the diversified enjoyments of intelligence itself. Here are a couple of ideas that can expand your mental horizons and increase your memory recognition.

Travel is one of the easiest hobbies people can undertake. Travel feeds the mind with an entirely new set of provocations, which forces your mind to do conductive problem-solving. For instance, when you travel you need to figure out train times, bus times, currency conversation, speaking foreign languages, geography, etc. You can probably see how travel correlates with memory. For instance, you most likely retain the experiences and pleasures of a vacation to a foreign language. Think of the last time you went somewhere new. Where did you go? What was it like? What did you do there? Just thinking about your past travels can trigger memory recollections.

Another example that can feed your mind with a new set of experiences is trying out new recipes. You can practically recollect the flavors of a new and extravagant dish. For example, do you remember what you ate for breakfast this morning? Chances are you do. Can you evoke the flavors in your mouth without any food in your mouth? Maybe yes, maybe no. But the point is, food can strike a nerve in your memory prompting you to recall it.

You can also recollect recipes that you have prepared routinely for several months or days. For instance, you probably can cook scrambled eggs without using a cookbook. Why? Because you already cooked scrambled eggs numerous times before that it's already stored in your memory. Professional chefs and bakers are especially good with this. Once you prepare a dish long enough, it will be permanently stored in your memory.

More examples include skydiving, freefalling, and parachuting, as it exposes your mind to an entirely new structural awareness which is completely unfamiliar to natural living.

How about trying out a new video game? When you play a new video game, you expose your mind to an entirely new and original virtual word that is different in reality. It adapts your mind to learn the controls, to learn the objectives, and to overall learn how to play the game.

You can attempt on learning a musical instrument. For beginners, I recommend you learn how to play the piano first as it is quite easy. You can use online guides and piano books to give you a start. Don't be afraid, try it and see how far you can go.

The same goes for learning a foreign language. Your memory is especially good in learning in a language completely unfamiliar to your mind. How about Spanish? Russian? German? Japanese? Mandarin? Or even Latin? Latin is especially difficult but worthwhile at the same time as it forces your memory and brain wholly.

You can also learn magic tricks as well. You see countless examples of magicians showing off their tricks on talent shows such as American Got Talent. They show off their magic tricks without any notes but from sheer memory. Learn a couple of easy and simple magic tricks. You don't need to do anything highly complicated. The bottom line is that whatever new skill set or hobby you decide to embark upon, do it with great enthusiasm and enjoyment. More importantly, mastering skills and hobbies will undoubtedly enhance your memory retention dramatically without you even being conscious of it.

REPEAT WORDS ALOUD

This technique is so simple but so effective that you might already be doing it subconsciously! When trying to memorize something, it can help you reciting information out loud to yourself. By repeating material in a spoken voice for a couple of times, you are making yourself to give your undivided attention to the given piece of material. In addition, it provides you with more opportunities to retain and soak up the material. Believe it or not, for most people and for the most circumstances, reciting information out loud is the only method they need to retain a given fact, date, or name for the sake of storing it into the short-term and long-term memory. The moment you verbally express information you encode it under a process known as an auditory encoding for later recall. Go on and give it a little try! Find a simple fact and chant it out loud for at least five to ten times. Do it with articulation and with comprehension.

If you need to memorize a particular quote or formula, you can just repeat the idea or material to yourself word by word. Better yet you can rehearse the thoughts and information through your own terms. Doing this will help set up a much clearer understanding of the material being bestowed to you. The explanation behind this is when you recite something aloud, you secure it in two distinct human senses. At the most basic level, you have the physical sensations of the words and information through your mouth, your esophagus, your tongue, and your lips when articulating them. Secondly, you hear those same words. The result of saying and hearing the words works concurrently to stick the ideas and material in your brain.

The reading out loud is the most crucial for memory retention. You cannot cheat by reading the material over in your mind. This will seem to be far less efficient than using your physical voice and speech centers to produce a certain noise. You can easily trick your mind into believing you have retained the information when in reality, you haven't. But it's much difficult to trick your ears. Making noise works in relation as to creating pictures in mind. And is extremely effective for memory recall.

However, don't just read something out loud only once. Repetition is vital for memory retention. The further you repeat something, the more you are capable of recalling the essence of it. Why? Because repetition creates a flow through the neural trails of your brain, making the information much easier to locate in the future. Here is a modest exercise you can test out.

Repetition works the best when you recite the material in your own words. By rephrasing the information verbally and theoretically, you are compelled to work with the material and interact with them. This process is more active and less passive. For example, let's say you are required to remember what plate tectonics are. The online definition is: "a theory explaining the structure of the earth's crust and many associated phenomena as resulting from the interaction of rigid lithospheric plates that move slowly over the underlying mantle." Repeating this definition out loud is far difficult and time-consuming. Rather simplify it and try saying this instead, "Plate tectonics is the theory that pieces of Earth's lithosphere are in constant motions, driven by convection currents in the mantle." When you put complex information into your own words, it forces you to think about it much more carefully and attentively and understand the material.

When reciting information to yourself, it may also help to recite them in fun and interesting voices. Rather than simply reciting your material in a dull voice, try singing the information to yourself. Use any musical genre and musical style you prefer. If you are a fan of Frank Sinatra, try singing upbeat like him. If you are a fan of rap, you can try wrapping your information aloud.

Another thing that you can do to enhance this exercise is by making vocal impressions of famous people while reading aloud. This will make repeating information more engaging and interesting when retaining the information. Say your learning materials in easy impressions like Elmo, Barack Obama, Bill Clinton, the Cookie Monster, Peter Griffin, or anything else. You can recite your information acting like someone you know like a professor, a teacher, your parents, or your boss.

The bottom line behind this exercise is to repeat and recite. Repeat and recite. Repeat and recite. And to repeat and recite the learning material until it is permanently latched onto your long-term memory. For some, this method will be the only one they need. However, for others repeating aloud may not be doing the trick. Don't worry there are still more methods that can aid you.

CAPTURING MENTAL SNAPSHOTS FOR REMEMBERING EVENTS

Neuroscientists suggest that our brains work best when using mental snapshots together with the association of events. When you absorb information into your brain using mental snapshots and association, they can be retrieved in the future with far greater ease. You can considerably enhance your memory access by imagining pictures, diagrams, cartoons, senses, and events using these snapshots to depict relationship and connect information together. Associations within theoretical and conceptual concepts can be recalled more easily when they can be seen on the tablets of memory. The key is free control of your natural ability of imagination!

At the most basic level, you can better remember key moments of your life by consciously using your eyes and brains like a living camera, purposely taking mental snapshots while events are happening. When you do this, you are directing your full concentration on the moment before you, thus encouraging the formation of stronger, clearer memories.

In the world of today, we are seemingly infatuated on the hype for capturing our most precious memories through digital cameras which are then uploaded to social media. Physical snapshots can help you retain information. However, if you have lost the image it will be difficult pulling it back up. Technology only goes a far way with pictures. If you learn how to process images and hold them in the back of your head, you can draw them up at any time, at any place. Here is how you can take a mental snapshot.

Let's take for example that you want to store the moments of a friend's wedding ceremony. First, you will observe attentively at the scene unfolding before your eyes. Keep your head still and scan the scene with great focus and concentration. Observe each moment of the ceremony. The bride and groom are walking down the lane, them exchanging kisses, and them cutting the wedding cake. Be aware of the atmosphere. What is everybody wearing? What is everybody doing? What were the conversations taking place? The best man's speech? Take note of the smell. Don't just think it or observe the events unfolding, but swallow in the sights and sounds of every moment of the ceremony. To take the photo, blink slowly once with your gaze locked on the scene. Imagine that you are pressing the button to snap the picture. Imagine the auditory clicking as the event is being reserved in your brain.

Next, go to your mental photo album and review the picture you have just photographed in your eye of the mind. If you make every effort to make a strong mental impression of this scene, the likelihood is that this photograph will be stored in your visual long-term memory, for recall for a later point in time. However, you shouldn't exert yourself and overdo it by taking a snapshot of every moment. Always focus on the quality rather than the quantity. Take mental images only when you seem it's imperative.

You can also recall complex abstract information using mental snapshots as well. The idea for this is because when you create a mental image of a concept, you effectively hold the information in another region of your brain, the visual cortex. Since visual information is connected with a different region of the brain from the area that deals with verbal information, this helps enhance your understanding to recall that information at another point in time. Let's give a practical example to illustrate this technique a little bit better.

Scientific principles and laws are often difficult to recall, but with mental pictures, it can come in effortlessly. The Second Law of Thermodynamic affirms that the sum entropy of an isolated system can only increase progressively. In layman's terms, the laws of thermodynamics explain the connection between thermal energy, heat, and other kinds of energy, and how these forces can change matter. If you wish to remember this law, imagine a LEGO death star all put together. If you put the LEGO death star in a box and shake it, will it construct the death star? Of course not, shaking a box filled with LEGOs will not put the pieces together in the exact precise structure. So, the Second Law of Thermodynamics states that if you place LEGOs in a box in a state of adequate entropy and shake it.

Then the probability of the LEGOs ending up in a state of higher entropy is higher than the probability of winding up in a state of lower entropy. Simply, you will most likely result in a pile of LEGOs than for you to end up with a fully assembled LEGO Death Star. Using this method, you will be able to combine both the Second Law of Thermodynamics with the visual representations of a LEGO death star in one simple, easy-to-remember mental snapshot.

However, on the other hand, if you are trying to recollect the precise details of a novel, try to imagine the characters and scenery in considerable detail. Rather than snapping a mental photo, image, or painting, you can produce a short movie or scene in your head featuring all the characters in a key situation described in the book! This can especially be used in the case for books adapted to movies. However, most movies always don't stay true to the book.

UTILIZING PLEASANT AND CHEERFUL MEMORIES TO STRENGTHEN YOUR MEMORY RETENTION

During the 1930s, psychologists hit upon the fascinating realization that negative memories diminish much faster than positive ones. Why? One explanation is our ability to recollect positive, uplifting, lovely, and charming memories at the same time abandoning negative memories helps to keep your mind happy and strong with a generally positive attitude on life. We remember pleasant or unpleasant events and information much better than impartial ones. This is because of emotional enhancement of episodic memory which is connected to the amygdala in neuropsychological research. The amygdala looks as it is accustomed the strength with which we recall conscious memories of events in accordance with the degree of emotional importance, despite whether the emotion is pleasant or unpleasant.

This discovery may not seem like rocket science. Most of us appear self-evident that we usually remember the more pleasant and enjoyable aspects of our experiences more than waiting for a taxi to pick you up. For example, you can easily recall the time you spent vacationing. Can you remember the relaxing and comforting days you spent exploring or can you remember the long hours spent waiting for your plane flight at the airport? Scientists refer to the mind's sifting of positive and negative from neutral experiences as Fading Affect Bias or FAB for short.

Later on, you will learn more advanced mnemonic techniques which will make use of mental imagery. Such imagery can be as vivid and sensual as you like. Above all, the mental representations should try to remain positive and upbeat as possible to achieve long-term memory recall. As a general rule of thumb, the brain tends to recall the positive and discard the negative memories over time, and so facts, information, concepts, and ideas connected to the negative metaphors will also be diminished away before you have the opportunity to store them in your long-term memory.

A study carried by the University of Limerick wanted to prove whether Fading Affect Bias was truly universal, despite cultural and environmental circumstances. The research was studied based on a diverse set of ethnic groups. What they found was that despite your cultural background and despite your environment context, the faster declining of unpleasant memories is not rare. It's not a spectacle that humans are capable of taking in negativity while at the same time holding an overall positive outlook on life. This is something which is seemingly hard wired into our brains, and it's something you can take advantage of.

So, the bottom line seems to be that we lean towards to removing unfriendly memories and remembering pleasing ones. By extension, associating information with happy and pleasant ideas or imagery it can help you retain information better and save it from the brain's non-aligned waste removal process which is always occurring in the background.

Use the mental connection of pleasant imagery to remember difficult to remember information. If you have a tough time recalling birthdays, you can still use this technique. Imagine yourself at a friend's birthday. Imagine yourself enjoying a gratifying piece of birthday cake. Imagine yourself handing the person a thoughtful birthday gift and watching their face glowing up with delight. After you absorb the moment, associate the experience with the specific memory you wish to recall. It may be unusual, but the association of both pleasant imageries with literal information will provide you much better recall than attempting to remember the information in seclusion.

When resorting to your mental imagery, try to exaggerate certain aspects and features of the image, as if it were a caricature. You can also give movements to your images, acting as if they were a movie in your head. Creating vivid images through these two simple methods will help settle them in your short and long-term memory much better. And whenever you use imagery in any associated memory techniques remember to make them as powerful and as imaginative as you possibly can.

HOW YOU CAN USE HUMOR TO BETTER YOUR MEMORY

Laughter is the best kind of medicine. As a matter of fact, there's a huge appeal for humor in all things you see today. Millions and millions of dollars are financing the production of funny television shows, comedy movies, YouTube videos, stand-up comedy, and even products. Laughter can make any situation, despite their surrounding contexts and circumstances, more bearable and even enjoyable. When we laugh, we are engaging in a social interaction that assists us to bond with our fellow human beings. As a physiological phenomenon, laughter consists of the contraction of the facial muscles, respiratory and laryngeal muscles. However, the question remains. Can laughter aid us in improving our memories?

Amazing enough, research suggests that laughter could improve memory in both visual and verbal tasks. The theory behind this claim is that an unusual stimulus, such as laughter, has the effect of standing out more than more accepted stimuli. Amusing and comical situations are naturally incongruent and direct increased levels of attention towards them. Another explanation suggests that comedy increases the arousal and activation of the sympathetic nervous system, which has a positive upshot towards memory

The emotional response to a joke will serve to improve your memory retention because the amygdala is being stimulated. This is the region of the brain that plays a crucial role in modulating memory consolidation. There is an increased response of the sympathetic nervous system, and this also serves to influence your ability to remember words, ideas, concepts, information, and details. This is the reason why the advertising and marketing industry spends tons of dollars to create humorous advertisements because humor promotes memory retention and recall.

As good as it is to share a laugh in order to aid our memory retention and recall. What kind of specific techniques can you use to spread laughter for greater memory recollection? A method that works efficiently, particularly in learning a foreign language, is using comic mnemonics. Take the following as an example:

To remember the Spanish word **abrir (to open)** think of the phrase **Abr**acadabra <u>**open**</u> *the jar right now!*

To remember the Spanish word **alcanzar (to reach)** think of the phrase **Al** *cannot* <u>**reach**</u> *the toilet paper.*

To remember the Spanish word **almorzar (to eat lunch)** think of the phrase **Al** *wants to eat lunch up in space.*

To remember the Spanish word **mirrar (to look)** think of the phrase **Mir**anda **looked** intensely at the talking **mir**ror.

There are countless more examples like these. Be creative and make some of your own! Please note, that the examples above are not plain and simple mnemonics. They are comic mnemonics because they exaggerate things out of the ordinary and are absurd, unnatural, and humorous mental concepts will make your mind sit up. Comic mnemonics are not particularly meant to send you rolling on the floor laughing.

Otherwise, how possibly can you learn? This fun little method is only designed to help people learn how to remember any fact through a fun and funny manner.

As a matter of fact, the odder the joke, the better. This will make your brain's pleasure centers spark. The more the subject can relate to you on a more personal point, the easier it allows you to file the information away and recall it at a later point in time. In reality, nobody knows this method better than advertising executives. If advertisers make their advertisements way too funny, the ad itself will not be remembered and not the product associated with it. All they'll be able to remember is the joke itself. It's therefore crucial to not overdo it with the comedy in your learning strategies.

Many teachers and professors have realized how effective humor can be to enhance their memory retention and cognitive abilities. To them, humor is crucial for the student's engagement and participation in studying. There is no better way to gain the better advantage and captivate your attention than twisting words and adding a joke here and there. Some ways you can use humor in your learning activities include:

BEING WEIRD: There's absolutely nothing more exhilarating than being weird and absurd. Think of weird scenarios and associate them with your material to retain them more. Remember, the more absurd the information is, the more you'll let your brain think about it, thus storing it.

USE VOICES: When you are learning, try different voices. As we talked about earlier, repeat your learning material through different vocal impressions. Changing the pitch of your voice can wake your brain and look for a giggle. You can even try to change your voice imitating someone you find funny in particular. For example, using Mickey Mouse is a childhood favorite and popular. Perhaps impersonating some well-known comedians such as Jim Carrey, George Carlin, Ricky Gervais, Louis C.K., or perhaps anybody else who can easily make you laugh.

You can also pro-actively seek out the elements of humor in any given topic or subject. Take the study of history for instance. You can look at newspaper cartoons on political topics that can be a fantastic way to incorporate laughter into your more serious legitimate study and a good way to experience how historical people viewed current affairs comedically during their day. Seek out the humor in any learning situation to binder those boring facts into your long-term memory!

RETROACTIVE INHIBITION AND FORGETFULNESS AND WHAT TO DO AGAINST THIS

Memory researchers and psychologists refer to two terms which are called **proactive inhibition** along with **retroactive inhibition. Proactive inhibition** results in people disremembering recently acquired information due to the intrusion of older memories. **Retroactive inhibition** happens when recently acquired information makes the memory centers forget older memories and information.

Proactive inhibition takes place because the recent information which a person is trying to learn opposes what the brain has already know prior. This is often the case with older people who have fixed mental attitudes on specific attitudes and behaviors. When they finally try to learn something new, it is distressing because their accustomed memories and knowledge prevents them from accepting the new ones

On the other hand, **retroactive inhibition,** causes the human brain to forget older information. This occurs even though previously learned information remains stored in the long-term memory centers of the brain and is because the person's working memory is distracted with processing fresh information. The power to recall old information is somewhat reduced if that information is underused and if there is a ton of information being pressed on the brain. This often happens when trying to learn new things and then trying to recall earlier ones. Take for example when you try to create a new password. The new password retroactively affects with the old one, which is now incapable for you to recall instantly.

The theory of inhibition claims that interference happens when learning new things interact with old things, affecting the transfer of information between long-term memory and short-term memory. This suggests that information remains stored in the brain, but cannot be easily repossessed due to the competition with the fresh information. All very well, but what does this have to do with combining effective learning with other activities?

Let's take for example that you just learned how to graph a polynomial function (which is calculus). When you head back home, you decide to finish a novel you started earlier this month. You spend minutes absorbing all the fascinating details and context of the story. However, while you are enthralled by the story and soaking up all the details, you are at the same time, getting rid of the knowledge on how to graph a polynomial function. Thus, you will need to go over it again and again in the later future. This is the case of **retroactive inhibition** where new information (details of the novel) replaces, previously learned information (how to graph a polynomial function). This doesn't mean you should stop learning new things. No, of course not. But there is a better way of retaining the lessons of calculus and enjoying your book later.

Let's take for instance that after the lesson on graphing a polynomial function, rather than heading home and reading your book, you decide to work on the homework assignment handed to you. Or let's say that after the lesson, you called a friend to discuss the lesson.

This will help your overall understanding of the subject as you combine other powerful memory techniques, including comprehension, vocalization, and social recollection of information. And later on late at night, before you fall asleep, you are still replaying the lessons in your mind, thinking of other problems perhaps. Once you fall asleep, your subconscious mind goes to work contemplating over the key points of polynomial function graphing and storing them in your long-term memory centers. By the time you wake up, your study material is now permanently stored and all because you didn't feed your brain with new information (the book) which will interfere and hinder the recall of the lesson. The next day you can enjoy the book as a reward from yesterday.

The key point to take away from this technique is not to learn something fresh and new after you just acquired important information. After an important lesson in class, don't replace the information with something else. Rather, study extensively and let it soak up in the mind until it is permanently enclosed in your long-term memory centers.

SHARE INFORMATION WITH ANOTHER PERSON

Share your knowledge and the things you learned with other people. As we talked about earlier, research suggests that reading material out loud significantly enhances the memorization process. However, if you combine both reading out loud with social interaction, you are engaging in different regions of the cortex in an amazingly cooperative way.

To take full advantage of this method, study in a study group or ask someone in your family to participate with you. Actors do this all the time when they are trying to rehearse their lines. They realize that studying with a partner who is pretending to be other characters make their practice all more appealing and their lines soak up into the memory much better. However, you may be asking yourself, why don't I just hire a tutor? The main difference between studying with someone and a session with a professional tutor is that tutors have a deeper knowledge on the subject than their student colleagues, and thus tutors have dominance when studying. When you study in a study group or with someone, you are learning information at the same time and at the same pace.

The usage of both study groups and study partners can be highly effective so long as certain important guidelines are being reviewed. For instance, only work with people who are as committed as you. It will not be very effective working with people who are unmotivated and uninterested in learning. In addition, you both should come to terms on how you work together and ensure that everyone in the group adheres to the agreed duties and responsibilities of the study group. Here are some tips to get the most out of studying in a group or with study partners:

When: Join a study group only once you have mastered the facts and information you need to know.

Why: The group's main goal is a laid-back discussion. Listen to your group partners, provide them feedback on their informational summaries, and supplement it with any facts which you know that they might have missed. This shared and contributive activity will help you exercise your senses, sight, hearing, and mouth/facial muscles, which are all helpful elements in memory processing and retention.

How: One effective system is for each member to prepare several essay questions in advance and then the group takes turns responding to them. If your group has prioritized accomplishments of accurate memorization, then a test one another using signals and hints to reach a common goal.

Where: Choose somewhere with not a lot of distractions, this will allow your group to handle the activity with your entire, undivided attention.

How Long: Typically, one to two hours devoted to quality group study is equivalent to studying six hours alone.

Who: Anybody is welcomed in a study group, as long as they understand the learning material being discussed and not very distracting. Make sure that each individual is there in the study group to discuss facts and ideas which have already been learned. The point of the group is to study, not to hang out and socialize. You can do that later. However, a studying group or studying partner should never replace individual study time. You must set the foundation at the lecturers, absorb the textbook contexts, etc. Study groups and study partners can drill each other, help one another, utilize newly acquired skills, clarify difficult points, present different perspectives on the material, and quiz each other out.

WRITE YOUR INFORMATION DOWN ON PAPER

One popular belief that college students, in particular, may pick up is that when they make an effort to take detailed notes on a lesson, their recall for their information is so good that they don't need to take a look at their original notes ever again. As a matter of fact, this belief is so popular that it may apply to everyone, specifically if you write something down it almost perpetually aids you to remember it much better! Our muscles are proven to have better memories than our brains and believe it or not, taking notes is a muscle activity. Writing things down with your hands make use of a different memory than listening or speaking. Using your arms, your hand, and your fingers is a physical action which will contribute to how much you remember. But, what is the reason behind this?

Well, the brain is divided into several different regions which process different sorts of information. They are different regions to process visual and auditory information, feelings, and emotions and verbal communication. Though these different regions communicate with one another, each of them holds their own duty and fulfills the requirements which need to be processed first. Hence, when you listen to a lecture, you engage that region of your brain which deals with listening and language.

This, in turn, passes certain sorts of information onto our memory centers. Though unfortunately, it doesn't do this in a very discerning fashion and quite often important bits of information are given the same classification treatment as trivialities. However, when you sit through a lecture taking careful notes, you engage that region of the cortex which handles spatial relations. This connection between the verbal building block of the information and the spatial relationship between pieces of data has the interesting outcome of filtering out the more unimportant information.

A study based on psychology students found that those who took notes were prone to remember a higher percentage of crucial information, while those who did not take notes remembered random and unorganized points made by the lecturer. This study confirmed what neuro scientists already suggests, that when we engage in the physical and mental act of writing down notes, we are participating in this process with a certain amount of mental ordering, evaluation, and categorization concerning the importance of the information bombarding us. You will be in effect of sorting through information from the unimportant ones to the important ones. And this serves as a filter and reinforce recall for the most important facts and diminish any trivialities.

However, what kind of note taking is the best? Will using a laptop to type your notes be as effective as writing by hand? Unfortunately, research suggests that taking notes on a laptop is not equivalent to writing them down by hand. You see, when you physically write something down, the brain actually believes the same way as pre visualizing the performance of some physical action or performance can enhance the skill with which it is then perform, and pre visualization is proven to be a powerful method used by actors, gymnasts, memory athletes, lawyers, students, and others.

So, when you attend a lecture, a seminar, a business meeting, or somewhere of value, always make an effort to take many notes while you listen to the information being presented to you. You will feel guilty when you come to study and find that you are missing a few key points that came up earlier.

The best practitioners of note taking do not just stop there, however. The most sharp-witted students and note takers continue to squeeze their notes into tiny and tiny bits while at the same time processing the knowledge and forging an understanding with last's week lecture material and the one before that. This process involves continual consolidation and reorganization on a weekly and monthly basis. Hence, prior to any important tests coming up, they make it a practice to do one last organization and consolidation, carefully fact-checking to ensure that their notes are completely accurate and precise.

MULTI-SENSORY PROCESSING TO RETAIN INFORMATION

The five senses (sight, hearing, touch, taste, and smell) are the keys to unfolding the world and the events surrounding us. Research has already proven that we rely massively on our five senses to comprehend new information. Think of your five senses as the learning doorways in your brain to process raw information and experiences. When you take advantage of using more than one sense when studying or learning, you amplify your information processing and memory retention. When you take advantage of using two or all of the five senses, you actually allow your mind to build more cognitive connections and associations with a given piece of information, concept, theme, idea, and even experiences. This authorizes information to bring about and salvaged from its cognitive repository in your brain's memory centers.

Now, everyone has their own particular style of learning, whether you are an auditory learner, a visual learner, or a tactile learner, or even something else. This means you will be better utilizing specified senses more than others. So, you must go through trial and error with using the multi sensory processing technique until you find something that works best for you.

YOUR SENSE OF SIGHT: It's self-evident that we need our sense of sight when learning anything new, especially when reading through books and online sources. After all, how can we possibly pick it up for our brains to process in the first place? To kick it up a notch, your sense of sight can be captured as reading or other learning activities that involve seeing, even if it is through words on a page, formulas, visual instructions, mathematic equations, diagrams, charts, etc. When you make use of visual stimulation, it will make you prone to greater memory retention.

To harness the full extent of your sight, try using color in your day-to-day learning activities. Rather than writing all your notes onto a dull white notebook, you purchased at a dollar store. Invest in a notebook that is colorful or one that stands out than every other one. As an alternative, you can try taking notes through different color pens or even highlight information in different color highlighters. Use a red highlighter to highlight the very important of information. Use a yellow highlighter to highlight the key points of your studies. Use a blue highlighter to highlight the things you need to go over and practice more on. These visual color signals can be an excellent way to fire up your visual cortex.

If you are learning difficult to remember subjects like the structure of a cell, which can be somewhat difficult to learn, there are many visual aids you can find through the Internet and google images. If you are seeking to learn the faces of famous philosophers, obviously, you could find pictures of them on google images and paste it into your notes. The more visual aids you include in your studying sessions and memory retention the better it will become to memorize things.

YOUR SENSE OF HEARING: As have gone earlier in the book, sound can play a paramount role in your learning experiences and memory retention efforts. For instance, we all heavily depend on our ears when e are listening to a lecture, an educational video, a podcast, or even an audio book. You can utilize sound into your learning experiences through a mixture of ways. One exercise is you can play orchestral and studying music such as Mozart that can be found on YouTube. These kinds of music are calming and soft-pedaled. It has been found that playing soft, relaxing music in the background while studying can boost your focus and learning abilities.

Another exercise that we went over is that you can repeat information out loud. When you come across information that you need to retain, repeat the learned information aloud. Doing this will force the cognitive centers to take notice of the material on three different sensory levels, which are visual, speech, and hearing.

YOUR SENSE OF TOUCH: Everybody is tactile learners, whether you are mainly an auditory or visual, there is still some tactile learning in you. It's human nature to reach out and touch things and to feel things which catch our attention. Obviously, touching doesn't seem to be much help when it comes to retaining information or in factual-based learning, but you can still make use of it. Here is one effective way:

Squeeze an anti-anxiety reliever ball whenever you study. Research indicates when you crunch a stress ball, it can actually aid your ability to remember information. Before attempting on memorizing information, squeeze an anti-stress ball with your dominant hand. When you need to remember a certain piece of information, squeeze the ball and take a breather. This easy exercise will fasten the material in your sense of touch and double your sensory input following the raw memory.

YOUR SENSE OF TASTE: Ever heard the phrase, 'what my childhood taste like?' Studies have proven that your sense of taste can bring up flashbacks and even information that can improve our very own memory retention. Let's take an example how you can combine taste and your history lessons. Have you ever thought about what people throughout history ate? When you are studying Native American culture, think about the foods they ate to survive? You can easily google Native-

American recipes through the Internet that and associate the taste of the foods with facts about their culture. If you associate these new and unfamiliar tastes with any sort of information, it can drastically help you retain it much better! For instance, to associate information with your chemistry class, do a little experiment and cook dinner. When you sear and brown meat it undergoes a physical reaction that you later can connect to facts.

Correspondingly, you can lay out predetermined scientific reactions using food like boiling eggs, cooking meat, and boiling uncooked pasta. When you cook food, it can also serve as a fun and enjoyable social activity after a lengthy studying session. For example, it will give you the opportunity to mutually review notes or relate what you have learned with other people.

YOUR SENSE OF SMELL: Your sense of smell is one of the most powerful sensory instruments that you have at your disposal. Why? Because smell is directly connected with the pleasures centers of your brain, we tend to subconsciously associate with favorable aromas and then connecting them with the information we learned. Smell creates strong emotional connections between us. That's why when you sniff a particular fragrance, you often recollect precious memories from the past. If you are learning herbology, find some samples and breathe in the scent to retain facts about them.

You can also use the sense of smell to enhance your studying environment. For example, during your studying sessions, spray air-freshener or light scented candles to please your nose and to boost your learning and memory performance.

DON'T CROWD YOUR INFORMATION WITH INFORMATION

Exposure to too much information is a present-day problem in this frantic society. However, it does not make it any less real than any other problems we deal with. If you find yourself become exhausted, without energy, or unmotivated, then this may be a reason for memory loss.

Going beyond the boundaries of what your memory can make room for deteriorating the capability and quality of cognitive function. Once you constantly overload your brain with too much information and data, the brain will lose parts of its processing abilities. Additionally, by oppressing the circuits, you lose the significant time of inactivity that promotes optimum cognitive performance. When the brain is crowded with too much information, it doesn't receive the rest it requires. The result is deficit communication in both short-term and long-term memory as it is interrupted by overextension.

When you squeeze in excessive information to your brain, it can take its toll. Studies show that most of us have experienced the misfortune of cramming for examinations, bucking up by countless cups of caffeine which sets our hearts running with every new fact we try to force inside our head.

Today's students have an even tougher time of it. Not only are they afflicted by the common syndromes such as unusual sleeping patterns, stress, poor diet, smoking, and alcohol consumption. Many people live in a province which is completely dominated by the Internet and social media platforms. Facebook, Twitter, and Instagram all encourages short-term gratification and promotes procrastination. The consequence for this is they will find themselves cramming thousands among thousands of facts into their brains the night of an examination. However, the main point is that cramming not only doesn't work but is actually highly counterproductive for good memory retention.

A recent study conducted by the University of California discovered that when you expand your information over a longer period, this will deem more effective than last minute studying of the material. Researchers found that during cramming sessions, people regularly mistake understanding with facts with knowledge of them. In actuality, the brain is tricking us into believing that we've memorized something when in all reality, we've done no such thing. The main idea to keep in mind is that familiarity is not remembering!

When we go over the same material for hours and hours, it's simple to convince ourselves that we've stored it in our long-term memory because every bit of information evokes a sense of familiarity which feels refreshing and gratifying. Each time we reread the same piece of information our brains intensify at familiar parts of information releasing chemicals which reassure us that we have fed the information into our long-term memory. However, the act of just recognizing something is in no way the same as the ability to remember it from scratch without optical aid.

Visual memory is defined by the easiness with which information passes through the sensory vicinities of our brain like the visual cortex if you are gawking at your study notes. On the other hand, memory recall is maintained by a different system of brain regions including the frontal cortex and the temporal lobe. These areas of our brain help organize together and can recreate memories from specific signals. The fact that your visual cortex is processing the study notes after six consecutive hours of cramming has no bearing on whether the memory centers of your brain are going to be able to reconstruct the memory later on!

Reviewing your study notes for hours is simply not enough to seal information into your memory. You must build up this practice with more enveloping and proactive habits as well. One way to encrypt information more profoundly into long-term memory is to create diagrammatic notes such as mind maps or concept maps. These visual aids spark comprehension and memory retention much better than simple bullet points. Sometimes, study notes and books can be too wordy for their comprehension and memory retention to bear.

For easier to remember information, try encrypting information down to a single key word or key phrase. This will help bring about the recall of larger chunks of information. Handwriting your study notes and rewriting them can also help your memory latch onto information and it also has the additional benefit of getting into the practice of writing rapidly during an examination. For example, computers have largely impaired this beneficial skill. Typing on computers can be sometimes bad because it tends to create distractions and increase the chances of procrastinations.

Researchers recommend that if you are presented with the only date in which to study, it's favorable to choose a day which is close to when you first learned the material than when you take the exam – but not too close. For instance, if you have a calculus lesson on Monday and a quiz next Monday, you should study on Wednesday for optimal memory retention. Tuesday is considered too early, and Sunday is way too late. The optimal time between two study sessions is about 10 percent of the time between the second study session and the examination. In other words, if you want to remember something for a year, you should wait about one month before you begin to review what you learn.

STUDYING STRATEGIES FOR MEMORY UPGRADING

How many times have you read a book, went to class, learned something new, study for a test, only to find to your distress that you had forgotten everything you soaked up in only a couple of short days? Well, you're not the only person suffering from this problem. Well, the thing is, the average person fails to remember up to 80% of learned information within only 24 hours of receiving it. Shocking, right?

Whenever you fail to use the newly fresh information you've just obtained, it's all too common to disremember what you carefully sought out. Therefore, it's if you wish to remember information for the long-term, you not only need to take detailed notes while you're learning, but you also need to study the things you learned. People can drastically increase the amount of information they retain once they start studying their learned information. It's common practice that we learned all the way back in grade school. Since elementary school, we had to study math, English, writing, science, and social studies, etc. The more we study, the more we remember, that's common knowledge. The same logic applies to any scrap of information.

If you choose not to study the fresh information, regardless of how methodically you have learned it initially, you will be prone to forget this information as time passes. Even after a few short days, it's common only to be able to recall a tiny portion of what we learned just the other day. To avoid misremembering things, you must transfer critical information from the short-term memory to the long-term memory, which is a process that takes time and effort. Reviewing and studying pieces of information is one of the most powerful and most effective approaches to accomplish this. In this section, we will take a look at some of the most highly effective studying strategies to recall any piece of information swiftly.

STUDYING STRATEGIES TO REVIEW INFORMATION EFFECTIVELY:

Here are some of the most highly-effective studying and reviewing strategies that you are free to use. Try not to ignore them and do your best to implement them in your studying routine.

STUDY YOUR INFORMATION RIGHT AWAY: Once you acquire the information you need to recall for the long-term, you should study it right away. You can begin by spending a couple of minutes reviewing the information at the exact moment when you learned it. Through this method, you are confirming that you have understood the contexts of the information and you save yourself the time to relearn it when you come to check it again sometime later in the future. While you are studying this information, make sure you do it with comprehension and with efficiency. If you simply do not have the time to go over this information, write down simplified notes and take a look at them when you have the time.

REVISE THE INFORMATION THROUGH YOUR OWN WORDS: Rewording and revamping fresh information is a fantastically efficient way to retain information. This way you are putting the information in a way that is more understandable for you. At first, it may come off as a bootless errand, but revising your learned information can reinforce the things among your short-term memory. Studies have proven that the simple act of revising your notes allows you to clarify your deeper expertise of any given subject matter.

THE PLACE YOU REVIEW CAN MAKE ALL THE DIFFERENCE: Where you study can either improve or worsen the quality of your studying session. Some people make the awful mistake of studying at a place that doesn't support productivity and focus. Most people attempt to study in a noisy place like their family room, the bus, parks, and other places surrounded by distractions and noise. You may choose to study in your room, but make sure you reduce or remove all sorts of distractions. Turn off the sounds and notifications on your computer, television, and phones. Also, if you are living with anyone, tell them to keep the noise down as you are going to study. You can also use any kind of quiet and relaxing place to focus and study your information. A library, a coffee shop, or a quiet room with no distractions are some locations you ought to test out.

SET TIME FOR YOUR STUDYING SESSIONS: Remembering any kind of information is a consistent process, if you want to switch information from the short-term memory to the long-term memory, it's vital to study your information as often as you can. Do your best to establish and follow a regular studying schedule. When you begin, start off by writing down everything that you can recall about the information and compare them with your previous notes. This way, you can provide yourself with the foundation of what you know and what you don't know. This can also help rejuvenate your brain and memory.

GET ORGANIZED: Aside from all the benefits of being organized, when you have either an app or a notebook that can help organize all your responsibilities varying from homework, work-related duties, projects, examinations, and coursework, it just makes your entire life easier. One thing that you should have is a daily to-do list where you write down everything you need to get done for the day. Make sure that you put down a studying slot somewhere on the list and make arrangements when new things come your way.

PAY ATTENTION THE FIRST TIME: When your boss is telling you something very important for you to remember, give them only your ears. It's necessary to focus and evade from distractions when someone is talking from you. Use your active listening skills by focusing on all that is being said and taking mental notes in your head. When you do this, you make sure that you don't miss any crucial information.

ASK QUESTIONS AND FIND THE ANSWERS IF YOU DON'T UNDERSTAND: If you are in class and the instructor is talking about something you can't quite understand, ask to elaborate furthermore. To study and retain something effectively, you must understand it completely. If you can't find the answer to your question, the Internet is a vast place to find all sorts of answers to all sorts of questions.

STUDY WITH ANOTHER PERSON OR WITH A GROUP: Reviewing with other people promotes an interactive, positive, and productive atmosphere for everyone to work in. This can provide you the chance to see if you learned something along the way while helping and working with others along the way.

FINAL THOUGHTS: In conclusion, to retain what we learn, we must carry out information from our short-term memory to our long-term memory. One effective way of doing this is to make information something of importance for us to study it regularly. Once we study the information long enough and effectively enough, it will hinge to our long-term memory for us to recall in the later future. If we ignore the studying part, this can make information more prone to deteriorate over time.

HOW TO USE FLASHCARDS THE RIGHT WAY FOR EFFECTIVE LEARNING AND MEMORY RETENTION

Repetition is the key to effective learning and for improving your memory. Flashcards is an excellent way to use repetition in a fun and interesting fashion. Flashcards also come with a variety of benefits outside these things. They can be used for both learning, studying, and memory enhancement by people of various ages. Some of the advantages of using flashcards include:

They can be made at home with household items. Very easy to make.

They are inexpensive to purchase at stores.

There are online tools for you to use them for FREE digitally!

They can be reused over and over again.

They are completely mobile and can be taken anywhere

You can come up with creative ways to learn with flashcards.

It helps people stay focus on new learning concepts

It encourages repetition and therefore effective learning and memory enhancement.

Here are three primary reasons as to why flash cards can be so effective for you to use on an everyday basis:

FLASHCARDS ACTIVATES ACTIVE RECALL: If you take a peek at your flash cards and come up with an answer in your mind, you are activating an intellectual aptitude known as active recall. What this means is you are being compelled to try to remember the information, idea, or thing from the ground up rather than gawking in a workbook passively. This is beneficial to you as active recall has been scientifically proven to create stronger neuron connections where memory is involved. As a result of, flash cards can easily assist the progress of repletion, which can create multiple everlasting experiences and events.

FLASHCARDS HARNESSES YOUR METACOGNITIVE ABILITY: While you turn over the flash card to find the solution, you are competently asking yourself the question, "How does my answer compare against the right one?" You are also implicitly asking yourself, "So, how properly did I realize the information being asked of me?" This is what is known as metacognition, and research has proved that making use of metacognition to our day after day remembering duties tends to instill knowledge much more profound into your memory centers. Thus, giving more reason as to why flash cards are efficient.

FLASHCARDS PROMOTES CONFIDENCE-BASED REPETITION (CBR): Due to the fact flash cards exist in a free and uncollected manner, as opposed to being connected to a book or document, you may categorize these cards into various differentiating piles relying on whether and how frequently you study them again and again. This practice is known as confidence-based repetition (CBR for short). Confidence-based repetition has been proven through research to be one of the best approaches to learning anything and to increase your memory abilities.

So, how can we get the most out of our flashcards?

Flashcards are one of the most old-fashioned and famous learning tools for straightforward memorization. Sadly, the majority of people use them in the wrong fashion. The best way to work with flashcards is by creating and designing your own handmade deck, which engages the creative regions of your brain. Your handmade deck should not include bare dictionary definitions and online lookups that you've extracted from the Internet. You should take advantage of the opportunity of creating the cards to modify the information in your own words, forcing you to process the information. As we gone before, going over information through your own words can increase the chances of memory retention. Therefore, getting to know the learning method starts without delay. When you are processing the information, you are creating thoughts and ideas in a pattern which has more meaning to you. This will help you in retrieving and reorganizing information in a fashion that strengthens your memory abilities. If you don't have the time or materials to create handmade flash cards, try downloading the app Quizlet or other flash card apps on your mobile device. There you can create an account and create your own deck of cards for you to use more digitally.

Then, once you have finished creating your deck, take a look at them whenever you have small periods of downtime. Try this in preference of checking your social media, checking your emails, or internet surfing. Always take advantage of your flash cards when you have a couple of minutes to kill. Since they're small, you may take your deck of flash cards with you anywhere you go. Use different strategies throughout this book to get the most. Don't zip through your deck of cards, take some time and have fun trying to think about the solutions. Don't make the mistake of cramming one large session with your flash cards, we've already covered how cramming is anathema to good memory technique, all you're doing is impairing your learning, so make sure to take small bites. The premiere way is to have impromptu, 15-minute periods while you're looking forward to the motivation to work. Likewise, a without difficult-digestible 30-minute consultation between classes or over lunch is recommended than pulling an all-nighter. Not only are you using your time much more productively, but you're memorizing with extra thoroughness and perception.

Organize your flash cards into separate piles depending on how well you've mastered and memorized the information. Nobody can retain every piece of information in a deck of flashcards equally well, so you shouldn't group all your cards into one gigantic pile which you then mindlessly flip through. Do your best to engage with the content and ask yourself the questions aloud and spend numerous minutes trying to recall the correct answer. Don't move on automatically when you are using the flash cards; you'll simply be wasting your own time. When you've been through the pile of cards several times, sort through and distinguish those that need additional work and study.

Flashcards are a reachable match for learning and memorizing; they are not anything that equates to its efficiency. Wherever possible, you should attempt to master brand new ideas and concepts using traditional learning strategies or by asking questions. But, when you need to check and access the materials you've already discovered through these standard methods, flash cards can become one of the best ways for doing this.

HOW TO USE MENTAL MODES FOR BETTER MEMORY

Mental models, also known as situation models, are mental representations of some state of occurrence in the real world and they serve as cognitive simulations of real events. When you read a passage, mental models help the situation through words and not the words itself. Mental models are often deeply complicated reorientations containing different kinds of information.

The spatial, temporal information systems define the framework of the events being explained, plus signs which serve to represent objects like people, animals, things, or ideas. These signals often have properties describing things like their physical characteristics, names, or emotional conditions and they are picked up by a network of structural relationships that define their spatial relationship to one another. Let's take for example that a horse and its equestrian are at a stable. In owner relationships, the equestrian and the horse are visitors of the owners of the stable and so on. However, these mental models are not established in cement but are vulnerable to change, for the simple motive that things in words and the actual world tend to transform gradually, following momentary development, and connection. But you may be asking yourself, how can mental models help you?

Well, mental models are crucial in the process of comprehension, understanding, and memory retention. When you read something through words, you create three various sorts of mental representations, which are:

VERBATIM MODEL relates to what you read or heard, which is usually hastily lost unless there is some reason to remember the exact sequence of words. For example, you need to remember the precise sequence of words to tell a joke or for the lines of a movie or play. But you don't need to remember the exact sequence of words to answer objective questions.

ABSTRACT REPRESENTATIONS, otherwise known as proportional text base, which is a partially visual representation of the idea elements being reached out. For instance, the sentences, "The horse is in front of the stable," and "the stable is behind the horse" would both correspond to the same propositional representation. Abstract representations are usually forgotten less rapidly.

MENTAL MODE is the final and most conceptual of all three, which is a referential representation of the events being described. Basically, the mental model is a representation of what is being communicated. The verbatim and text base levels which anticipate it are simple representations of the message itself but can also serve as the platform from which the mental model is built.

Mental models are a needed element for memory enhancement! Eventually, after some time, the mental model is the precise representation of reality that will control your memories. Mental models include both the given information as well as the information inferred from the verbatim and text base levels, and gradually, it becomes progressively difficult to unscrambled these two, the given and the inferred. Mental models contain knowledge and assist us in the formation of fresh knowledge. At first glance, it gives us the impression that we are invigorating these mental models without effort because most of the time we're not even alert we're doing it. Down the line, however, it's clear that our minds are working hard to create these representations. One instance of this is playing chess with another to determine whether the pieces tag a checkmate. This is an element of mental models; some require more brain processing power than others. Determining whether a set of chess pieces will activate checkmate in only three moves will be quite difficult.

Research suggests that the human brain can generally hold up to seven objects at the same time within their working memory. This cognitive computing power has a straight impact on our processing of mental models. Well, how can we use mental models or recreations of reality to help us in our memory-related duties? Here is some advice:

Start your day by visualizing a successful studying session, and do it before you begin the study session. Set aside five to ten minutes for visualizing. Be as descriptive as you possibly can, thinking of all the steps you will take, such as reading the sections and completing exercises planned for that day, along as reviewing the material after that. Prepare which parts of the day's study session you will find particularly challenging, which will help prepare you for any problem. Then, imagine yourself at the end of your day experiencing the joy at having reviewed the required material and understanding/remembering all the main points.

Celebrate small success every day, instead of throwing one huge party after you take a test. This will improve your motivation and increase positive energy. Finally, take a moment to imagine how you will treat yourself later as a prize for the countless hours you study. Rewards might be watching a movie, going to the beach, or going out for dinner with friends. When you use positive mental models to reap the more positive results in our personal reality, we give memory retaining and our cognitive skills a hyper-boost.

TAKING ADVANTAGE OF YOUR ENVIRONMENT FOR YOUR MEMORY

Believe it or not, in some cases you don't need to practice these highly-complicated techniques to improve your memory retention. In fact, all the tools you need to improve your memory can be right there in your environment, your home, or your office. You can use simple everyday household objects as active memory enhancements to remind you of tasks and other things you need to recall.

Additionally, you can also use the items of your personal environment. This includes the things regarding your physical body and attire. Let's take for instance, that you want to remember an important dentist appointment. To remember the dentist's appointment try wearing a watch on the wrong wrist. When you peek at the watch to check the time, you will be continually reminded that you have something important to do later on. After you visit the dentist, you can switch the watch book onto the right wrist.

Another quick and easy method for recalling something s to place an ordinary, everyday kitchen appliance in a strange position right before you sleep. This could be your microwave, your toaster, your coffee pot, salt shakers, etc. When you wake up the next morning and prepare breakfast, you will take record of the misplaced objects. If you placed the bowls on top of the refrigerator, you would be immediately reminded that there is something you need to remember as you reach for the bowls. Do remember to return the bowls back to their original place once you've finished whatever it was you were supposed to do. For instance, after you take your daily medicine, place all the bowls back to where they belong and continue with breakfast.

However, the actual trick to memory retention is associating the object being used as a memory jogger with the specific piece of information you need to remember. So, rather than using bowls, use coffee pots if you make coffee every day. You can associate your daily morning coffee with medicine as it can remind you to take your pills before you enjoy a cup of coffee.

If you choose to associate an appliance that lacks any association with the given fact, it can be very difficult to remember the things you were supposed to recall. For instance, if you decide to misplace a spatula to associate your medicine intake, you will most likely forget where you placed the spatula and forgot to take your daily medicine supplements.

Another example includes setting a book in front of your door if you need to remember to turn in a paper or homework assignment. When you see the misplaced item, it will immediately shake your memory in a purposeful manner.

Your entire house is literally filled with objects which can be misplaced or laid out in ways to remind you of crucial tasks and events. And even better, if you remember the things you were supposed to remember, you can just place the item back to its original position again. Here are a couple of ideas where you can harness your environment to serve as memory bouncers:

Remove batteries from your television remote

Place your phone charger somewhere else

Place your wallet or phone in the other side pocket of your pants from where you normally place it.

Place the pillows lengthways rather than sideways.

Put your keys on top of your lunch box inside your refrigerator. Therefore, you won't leave your house without your keys and lunch box.

Place sticky notes everywhere you can.

Flip a tissue box over, so the tissues are facing the floor.

Place toothpaste next to the dog food, so you don't forget to feed your dog and brush your teeth. Or the other way around.

Put the dog's bed or cage at the opposite area of the house.

Place brooms, mops, vacuums, dusters, and other cleaning appliances somewhere else than where you usually keep them.

Find other creative ways to practice the full extent of this technique.

HOW TO USE WORD LINKING FOR MEMORY RETENTION

Here we will learn how to memorize through word linking together the distinct pieces of information we are trying to learn. Otherwise known as the chaining method or the storytelling method, word linking is a highly-effective memory technique which works by mental projections of the things you want to memorize and linking these images together like a chain or a story. It all depends completely on your visualization and imaginative abilities.

YOUR FIRST ASSIGNMENT: You are going to remember a record of twenty random objects, first through your short-term memory, and then to your long-term memory. If this sounds difficult, don't worry. You are going to peek at each word and will be able to remember it easily.

First, we are going to memorize the list the classic way. Take a look at the words as many times as you want, recite it in your head, then look away and hastily jot down as many words as you can remember. It doesn't necessarily have to be in the precise order, just get these words in your head:

1. Box of Chocolates

2. Flowers

3. iPhone

4. Frying Pan

5. Bottle of Glue

6. Glasses

7. Bread

8. Lip Gloss

9. Trees

10. Money

11. Lightbulb

12. Bowtie

13. Tennis Ball

14. Squirt gun

15. Piggybank

16. Bullets

17. Jigsaw Puzzle

18. Pocketknife

19. Toy Robot

20. Popcorn

USING THE LINKING SYSTEM

For the linking system, you will first conceive a mental image of each object in your mind that is realistic but yet bizarre. Then, you will link the mental image in the list by having the objects reaching out with another. Be aware that the process of word linking may come off as difficult, but it is entirely easy and quick to use. Here is the linking system using the list from above. Read the list and envision each picture openly in your head.

BOX OF CHOCOLATES/FLOWERS: Imagine it's Valentine's Day and you are gifting your lover with a box of milky dark chocolates and a flower bouquet. Imagine your lover's reactions and the feelings in your head.

IPHONE/FRYING PAN: You are starving, but there's nothing to eat. You decide that the only thing left to eat is your iPhone. Imagine yourself heating a frying pan over medium0hgih heat and placing your iPhone on the frying pan. After two to three minutes, you flip the iPhone over like a burger and allow it to cook for another three minutes. Imagine the process and the result of cooking your iPhone.

BOTTLE OF GLUE/GLASSES: You just sat on your only pair of Gucci glasses. It's way too expensive to buy another pair, so you attempt to fix it using a bottle of glue. Imagine yourself gluing the broken pieces of the glasses together in hopes of repairing it.

BREAD/LIP GLOSS: Imagine yourself having a bottle of lip gloss nearby, and you decide to put the lip gloss to glaze the bread (as stupid as it may sound) Imagine the color of the lip gloss. What kind of bread is it? How does it taste? **NOTE:** As mentioned earlier, using more than one senses in your mental representations can increase the likelihood of you retaining it. As disgusting as it sounds, imagine yourself taking a bite of the lip-gloss glazed bread.

TREES/MONEY: Money does grow on trees … at least when it comes to your imagination. Imagine a huge tall wooden tree, but all the leaves are replaced with authentic hundred dollar bills. Imagine yourself at the tree attempting to pick some money or so.

LIGHTBULB/BOWTIE: Imagine yourself having trouble tying a bowtie. Until a light bulb light up above your head which suggests you have an idea. You went to the store and bought a clip-on and easy to put on the bowtie.

TENNIS BALL/SQUIRT GUN: Imagine an all-out deadly war. One faction uses tennis balls to throw and strike down their enemies. The other side uses squirt guns to shoot their enemies in their head.

PIGGYBANK/BULLETS: Imagine where you had a piggy bank and you collect bullets in there. When an intruder breaks into your home, you run to your piggy bank and shatter it to the ground. Bullets come running on the floor, and you pick up a couple of bullets to load your gun, ready to defend yourself.

JIGSAW PUZZLE/POCKETKNIFE: Imagine a scenario where you and a friend are completing a jigsaw puzzle, but the entire pictures make up a large pocketknife.

TOY ROBOT/POPCORN: Imagine where it's the future and you have your own personal toy robot popcorn machine. When it's time to watch a movie, you pull up an app on your phone to give the command to your toy robot. You ask the toy robot to make you some hot popcorn for you to enjoy with the movie. The toy robot does it willfully.

These are simple word linking examples that you can invoke in your mind to link these twenty items together for easy recall. You can ask someone to tell you a random set of objects or make your own to perform this technique right now. However, I think it's crucial that you know that these scenarios and visualizations were never meant to make sense. It's okay if you want two objects to be realistic or as fictional as possible. It's your imagination, and you can make it anything you wish.

As a general rule of thumb, it's generally best to use to follow the sequence than to choose the objects you prefer more. Your goal is to remember the whole list in its precise order, and your own subconscious will tell you which mental image is most effective for this. More importantly, don't allow yourself to become unmotivated if it takes you time to master the linking method correctly as this whole process is natural. Sometimes it can be a little bit embarrassing to imagine weird, absurd, odd, and offbeat scenarios. However, do realize that nobody will be able to see your imagination except for you. The main point is that this technique aids you to remember lots of different things with absolute ease. As in the case of every skill, memory techniques like word linking needs effort, time, and practice for your mind to get accustomed to. If you practice for at least five minutes a day, you will ultimately be able to create the necessary mental images and quickly link them together in your head in seconds.

The linking method is a really easy and simple way to learn and remember various pieces of information, especially if that information grant itself to being linked together. It doesn't require a vast amount of creative energy or time and is a specifically useful when merged into your everyday life. So, rather than writing down lists or relying on your phone, give your mind a workout by using linking imagery to recall grocery lists, activity lists, or work-related tasks. The great thing about linking imagery is that the mental scenarios you create will remain in your memory for a long time until the time comes to create a new one. This allows you to memorize things for the long-term, which would usually be entered into your short-term memory and be hastily lost.

CHUNKING INFORMATION FOR BETTER MEMORY RETENTION

Chunking information, or also known as going by parts is an easy-to-use dynamic method for grouping lists of things to help you retain them. The human brain can only process a limited measure of information at any given time. Therefore, grouping is necessary for this alone.

Additionally, when you group individual pieces of information into a more meaningful chunk, you are engaging in an active mental process known as organization, a key factor in memory processing. Research suggests that groups of three are the most effective and we habitually group phone numbers on this foundation because it's simpler for recall. You can chunk information into either light portions or group them into distinct categories. Let's go over the category method.

A list of items without any connection can be especially difficult to remember. Let's take this list of ten items as an example:

1. Cat

2. Pizza

3. Flowers

4. Spoons

5. Crayons

6. Butter

7. Piano

8. Sailboat

9. Giraffe

10. Oatmeal

To make memorizing simpler, try labeling each item in the list by category or type. For example: Foods (pizza, butter, oatmeal) Animals, (cat, giraffe) and Objects (flowers, spoons, crayons, piano, sailboat) Now all you need to do is memorize three food items, two animals, and five objects.

This method is especially powerful when you do grocery shopping as you can classify the various items that you need to buy as specified by what they are. For example, fruits, vegetables, dairy products, cereals, meats. This will not only aid you to manage your shopping list but also help you recall the individual items under each category. This will also help you complete your weekly shopping a lot quicker as well.

On the other hand, an alternative to the chunking method is you can separate your list by parts going by the initial letter of each word. Let's say that you need to buy milk, eggs, chicken, yogurt, and avocados (think of

M, E, C, Y, and A). When you are shopping at the supermarket, all you need to do is remember the letters, M, E, C, Y, and A. You can remember the letters through another method known as acrostics which we will talk about later. Once you've retained the precise letters to your memory, you will be able to recall the list going by each letter.

Chunking information, if you can recall, the example that amongst other things, you need to purchase four various sorts of vegetables. It will be easier for you to remember all of them. How often do you go grocery shopping only to forget one important ingredient for dinner? This simple method will help avert culinary dismay such as this. In fact, we already chunk information in long phone numbers or credit card numbers. This is the second variation on the chunking method which involves individual grouping items together into tinier component portions

For example, will it be easier to memorize 3259351845 or 325-935-1845? Let's say you've just been issued a brand-new credit card and you want to memorize the number just in case you lose it. Will it be easier to memorize 7832938325083923 or going by parts, 7832 9383 2508 3923? (NOTE: These are random numbers I came up on the spot, it's not a real credit card number)

Here's another example, it will be impossible for you to memorize a thread of numbers like 1861193919451981. However, if you add a space to every four numbers (1861-1939-1945-1981) now, you can see that those numbers are years and you can choose the key events in each year to help you remember the series of numbers. In this case, 1861 is the start of the Civil War, 1939 is the start of World War 2, 1945 is the year the United Nations was found, 1981 is the date Ronald Regan served as president.

Try the next chunking exercise. Here is an order of letters: XCGCACCTTGAACGAX. Can you chunk these letters into five easy-to-recall chunks? Give it a try. Here is how I did it. You resolve the chain into the following: GCC-ACC-TTG-AAC-GA is the letters between the XX which serves as bookends for the sequence of letters. These can be made to stand for the DNA codon table + GCC + ACC + TTG + AAC + GA + XX which takes their place either side of the letter-thread, simple enough!

HOW CAN RHYMING HELP REMEMBER THINGS?

Since our brains have a mind-boggling hearing space, word-rhymes can serve as a powerful aid to creating fresh memories and allows us to remember information more. Scientific research has proven a strong link between improved memory and the usage of rhymes, specifically those rhymes which are designed to separate rhymes.

In most cases, ordinary writing is tougher to remember than the rhyming lines of poetry. Rhyming and rhythmic memory methods offer two vital organizing factors for the memorizer: rhythmic pattern (another saying for "meter") and rhyming of the end word in the consecutive repetition of the rhythmic pattern.

Examples of how rhyme can help us remember things include Homer's "Odyssey" a lengthy book that many people were able to memorize due to the use of rhyme, rhythm, and repetition. Parents and nurseries have been making good use of this knowledge about word rhyme, rhythm, and repetition as an aid to recall. How did you learn the alphabet when you were young? Well, you learned the ABCs song which resembles the melody of the song, "Twinkle, Twinkle, Little Star."

Using a variety of common or nonsensical rhymes can help you store basic information to your long-term memory centers. For instance, there is the generally known mnemonic, "Thirty Days Hath September" which goes:

30 days hath September,

 April, June, and November,

All the rest have 31,

Excepting February alone.

Which only has but 28 days clear

And 29 in each leap year

Let's take another example that will help students of Latin remember unacquainted Roman Numerals:

I am a Roman soldier 1 (1 equals to I)

5 Victories I have won (5 equals to V)

X marks the spot where 10 comrades fell (10 equals to X)

Only 50 Lived to tell (50 equals to L)

100 more were Captured in war (100 equals to C)

Now we fight 500 Days more (500 equals to D)

1000 soldiers Marching on tour. (1000 equals to M)

Rhyme, rhythm, and repetition take advantage of our brain's astonishing ability to encrypt audio information and data. How about this popular rhyme for remembering the date where the Americas were founded by Christopher Columbus, which goes:

In 1492 Columbus sailed the ocean blue.

Or perhaps you want to remember a person's name you can sometimes connect the sound of their name to some other aspect of their personality. For example:

Deon is n**eon**

Bon**nie** is scra**wny**

C**lark,** the sh**ark**

P**aul** has a d**oll**

Charl**ene** is gre**en**

B**ob** is a bl**ob**

H**arry** is a f**airy**

D**aniel** has a sp**aniel**

And so on!

Additionally, advertising companies and lyricists have made tons of rhyming words. How many advertising jingles can you remember from your childhood or even from today? They are adding rhymes onto their products, candy, cosmetics, and food. Why? Because our memory is locked onto rhymes and jingles. The top songs on the radio are usually songs whose lyrics are easier to remember and those that rhyme. Creative students have taken advantage of using rhyme to remember often complex information.

Along with all these memory methods, when making memory rhymes or poems, it's not recommended to spend an awfully lot of time making them. The best ones are usually simple and come up on the spot. They are just an auditory aid for your ability to remember.

MUSIC TO BOOST YOUR MEMORY RETENTION

The same as any kind of word rhymes, music can be a mighty and effective instrument for storing information to our long-term memory centers. Scientific research suggests that these sorts of musical mnemonics work because they develop the brain to find patterns in information, creating in the process meaningful associations with frequently arbitrary information. Songs and music enable the mind to illustrate that information in different parts of your memory through sounds. To prove the efficiency in music as a tool for memory, just think of all the songs you can play in your mind instantaneously? How many songs can you sing on the spot? How many songs can you listen to your head without any sort of MP3 playing in the background? You may not be able to remember the specific name of the song or even the lyrics or artist, but you do know that you have heard that song before. More evidence includes the famous ear worm, where a song is glued in your head going around and around in your brain sometimes for an endless stream of days.

Jingles relate to music too. Jingle is a sort of rhyme, which has been used for centuries now. You can find jingles mostly in infomercials, advertisements, slogans, and catch phrases. The reason why jingles are heavily used to promote products is because advertising experts realized the fact that jingles and songs cause consumers to remember the commercial (thus, their product) more. Studies have proven that music enhances subject recall, unless the music is weird and make it difficult to remember. Simple lyrics and simple melodies are what make songs stick and work the best. If you make use of jingles the appropriate way, you can make them stuck in people's head for a very long time.

Memorizing information by applying it to musical songs is a method that almost everybody can take advantage of. It's not necessary to be specifically creative when you are making your own musical mnemonic. As a matter of fact, the simpler the song, the better. You might like to try applying your information to a nursery rhyme since most of these are archived within our long-term memory from childhood.

Likewise, try using one of your favorite or familiar songs instead. Sometimes the key information has already been made into music ready for use. Such example is remembering all the United States Presidents, which one innovative YouTuber replaced the lyrics to Yankee Doodle with the names of presidents.

Some students like to turn to Schoolhouse Rock songs when trying to retain facts about the Government and Political Science lessons to memory. Students who do this sometimes find themselves playing this song in their heads during testing, recalling the facts to hand with greater ease since they're just the words to a song.

You can also use the music as a background aid for greater relaxation, concentration, and recall without having to come up with your own rhymes, songs, or jingles. When you simply listen to music, it stimulates the hippocampus, the region of the brain that handles long-term memory storage. This means that by listening to a certain piece of information, you can evoke the relevant memories that you made while first learning the information.

However, do your best to avoid songs or musical genres which can be too noisy and rowdy or which have too much going on. Pick songs that are relaxing and soothing which you really can enjoy. Maybe songs that your mother or father used to sing to you when you were young. This will have the additional advantage of arousing friendly family memories of being safe, loved, and cared for. The combination of comfortable sensations and relaxing music will, in this manner, provide your memory recall an extreme boost. So, the next time you face the daunting task of retaining a lot of difficult facts to memory, make the process easier by using musical mnemonics and let those memories become archived.

THE NUMBER RHYME TECHNIQUE

Mnemonic number rhyme pegs are a without question a fundamental memory method to keep in your bag of tricks for recalling information. This method works by associating word pegs or number rhymes with information that you wish to remember in the future. A word peg is merely a mental hook on which you set about hanging the new information, and it serves as a reminder to help you recollect the knowledge later. It works like this, from each number from 1 to 10, you will assign an object whose name shared assonantal similarity with the number. A very common number-rhyme peg arrangement is right here, feel free to adjust it to your liking.

One rhymes with gun

Two rhymes with screw

Three rhymes with sea

Four rhymes with gore

Five rhymes with bricks

Seven rhymes with heaven

Eight rhymes with weight

Nine rhymes with wine

Ten rhymes with pen

Again, you can change this number-rhyme system to your liking, or you can use the example above.

In the example above or with your own exclusive number-rhyme system, make sure you commit it to your long-term memory as you will be using it from now on. Now, let's take for example that you need to memorize your shopping list:

SHOPPING LIST

1. Milk

2. Carrots

3. Soap

4. Jelly

5. Rice

6. Meat

7. Ice Cream

8. Mayonnaise

9. Cereal

10. Fish

You can connect and associate the **10-memorized number-rhyme pegs** with your **shopping list** by associating them in the following way. You can associate them in this fashion or in a way that relates to you more

To associate milk with the image of a gun, imagine opening your refrigerator looking for a carton of milk, only to find a gun in place of the carton of milk.

To associate carrots with the image of a screw, imagine yourself hammering down screws onto a large orange carrot.

To associate soap with the sea, imagine a large, blue, and bubbly soapy sea.

To associate jelly with the floor, imagine a scene where you dropped a jar of grape jelly on to the floor, and now it is everywhere.

To associate rice with bricks, imagine someone eating gore with a side dish of rice (can be a little gruesome to think about)

To associate meat with bricks, imagine yourself using a red brick as a mallet to flatten the meat.

To associate ice cream with heaven, imagine yourself dead and have gone to heaven, but heaven is actually ice-cream land!

To associate mayonnaise with weight, imagine somebody getting fatter and fatter as they continue to eat mayonnaise.

To associate cereal with wine, imagine yourself adding cereal into a bowl and rather pouring in milk, you pour in red wine.

To associate fish with a pen, imagine a celebrity signing their autograph using a pen onto a fish fillet.

These word associations were instantly made up, and most of them are goofy and flabby, but that's not the point. The point is to is whether the word association can aid you in recalling the target objects for the short-term all the way to the long-term. Now if using this memorable mental imagery associated with number-rhyme pegs, you are able to recall your shopping list for the next couple of days. The great thing about this specific technique is that it's dead easy to learn and begin using in everyday memory-related tasks. With some effort and practice, you should be able to come up and memorize any sort of list of 10 items in a matter of minutes. What's more interesting is that your memory of the list of targeted objects have a tendency to be far stronger than if you had just learned them. The minute you mastered this method you might want to examine with peg words from eleven to twenty, in which case you can use:

Eleven rhymes with Kevin

Twelfth rhymes with elf

Thirteen rhymes with screen

Fourteen rhymes with clean

Fifteen rhymes with queen

Sixteen rhymes with Sistine (i.e. Sistine Chapel)

Seventeen rhymes with string

Eighteen rhymes with Spring

Nineteen rhymes with sleeping

Twenty rhymes with penny

HOW TO IMPROVE YOUR MEMORY USING ABBREVIATIONS AND ACROSTICS

Using both abbreviations (or acronyms), and acrostics are two-related methods which are a fantastic tool for remembering a wide variety of objects, things, lists, sayings, and information. Acronyms are invented combinations of letters, each letter serving as a signal to imply an item that you need to recall. This harnesses the efficiency of the 'First-Letter Association Technique,' where you use the first letter of each text in a line of words you wish to remember and make a word or phrase relating to it. For instance, do you know the names of all five Great Lakes in the United States? Maybe you do, maybe you don't. However, you can use the first-letter association, HOMES, which translates to:

H stands for Lake Huron

O stands for Lake Ontario

M stands for Lake Michigan

E stands for Lake Erie

S stands for Lake Superior

Another example of first-letter association relates to your day-to-day texting. Here are a couple of most used examples:

LOL stands for 'Laugh Out Loud.'

TBS stands for 'to be Announced.'

IDK stands for 'I Don't Know.'

DIY stands for 'Do It Yourself.'

OMG stands for 'Oh my God.'

NaN stands for 'Not a Number.'

N/A stands for 'Not Available.'

BRB stands for 'Be Right Back.'

TGIF stands for 'Thank God It's Friday.'

POV stands for 'Point of View.'

ROFL stands for 'Rolling on the Floor Laughing.'

BTW stands for 'By the Way.'

AKA stands for 'Also known as.'

WTH stands for 'What the heck.'

TTYL stands for 'Talk to you Later.'

P.M. stands for 'after noon.'

A.M. stands for 'before noon.'

BC stands for 'before Christ.'

ASAP stands for 'As soon as possible.'

ETA stands for 'estimated time of arrival.'

P.S. stands for 'post script.'

More examples of popular acronyms widely used by most people include:

U.S.A stands for the United States of America

NATO stands for the North Atlantic Treaty Organization

STM stands for short-term memory

LTM stands for long-term memory

CIA stands for the Central Intelligence Agency

FBI stands for the Federal Bureau of Investigation

NBA stands for the National Basketball Association

EU stands for the European Union

AP stands for Advanced Placement

NASA stands for the National Aeronautics and Space Administration

These are simply some of the most effective memory aids available to us that we constantly use in our day-to-day life. And since we use them on a daily basis, it sticks to our long-term memory. Another example where we use in educating and math-related duties is 'PEMDAS,' this translates to the order of evaluation math equations:

P stands for Parenthesis

E stands for Exponents

M stands for Multiplication

D stands for Division

A stands for Addition

S stands for Subtraction

Using abbreviations are so effective because they focus our attention on assigning meaning to the learning material we are learning. They allow us to memorize more by memorizing less. As the examples above, where you memorize HOMES rather than five separate Great Lakes. Abbreviations also give us clues because memory recall always works with a little reminder, so knowing the first letter provides us the first letter of the name we're trying to recall. The First-Letter Association also lets us know when we've completed the memory remembrance test because if you match an item with every other letter on the record, you're essentially done, as everything you need to recall is confined in that abbreviation.

Now, how about, we create our very own exclusive acronym to the first letters of the object list from harnessing this very technique. Let's take for example that you need to remember these set of objects: book, apples, toy, water, ax, lamp, earphones, coffee, and salt. The abbreviation that these set of words make up is, "BATWALECS." This one can strain our creative minds a little bit. You can break this down and arrange the letters to something that makes a little bit more sense. But, if you act as if the abbreviation is just a normal peculiar word, it'll still be as effective.

To remember this abbreviation more effectively, try breaking it down and go by parts. With the first three letters being 'BAT,' imagine a vampire bat. With the next six letters, you can think of a whale where the c will remain silent. So, in summary, think of an unusual relationship between a bat and a whale. These abbreviations will first sound absurd and weird, but the weirder it gets, the more it sticks to your memory. Doing this will enable you to recall the abbreviation, "BATWALECS" easily and based on the abbreviation, you can then find your way back to the set of objects: 'book, apples, toy, water, ax, lamp, earphones, coffee, and salt,' in no time.

You have combined both abbreviations and grouping by parts with word linking and mental imagery in improving your memory. This is especially good as combining more than one memory technique can further your chances of improving your memory. Sometimes, however, a given acrostics simply doesn't

HOW TO USE ARCROSTICS

Sometimes, however, a particular acronym simply isn't capable for easy memorization. This is especially in the case of having a set of first letters that are lacking in vowel sounds. In this case, you can switch to a related technique to acronym known as acrostics.

Acrostics are very similar to acronyms except that instead of just remembering the isolated acronym, you create a whole new sentence from the first letters of a group of words remember than a long string of unrelated letters. You can easily invent your own acrostics. Here are some of the most popular acrostics in daily use:

To memorize the notes of the treble clef, use 'Every Good Boy Does Fine,' which translates to **EGDBF**.

To memorize the points in a clockwise compass, use 'Never Eat Sour Watermelons', which translates to North, East, South, and West. Acrostics really come in useful for much more complex lists of facts.

To memorize the order of taxonomy, use the mnemonic, 'Do Kids Prefer Cheese Over Fried Green Spinach", which translates to, Domain, Kingdom, Phylum, Class, Order, Family, Genus, Species.'

To memorize the seven essential amino acids, use the mnemonic, **"Pvt. Tim Hall"**, which translates to,

Phenylamine, **V**aline, **T**hreonine, **T**ryptophan, **I**soleucine, **H**istidine, **A**rginine, **L**eucine and **L**ysine

To memorize the order of guitar strings, use the mnemonic, '**E**very **A**verage **D**ude **G**ets **B**etter **E**ventually,' which translates to **E** string, **A** string, **D** string, **G** string, **B** string, and **E** string.

To learn the seven conjunctions in English, use '**FANBOYS**,' which translates to **F**or, **A**nd, **N**or, **B**ut, **O**r, **Y**et, and **S**o

Again, using our previous example from before, **BATWALECS**. WE could create the following simple-to-remember acrostics: "**B**ears **A**te **T**all **W**ooden **A**nimals **L**ike **E**very **C**at **S**ays."

CHAPTER 7: HOW TO REMEMBER NAMES AND FACES OF PEOPLE?

In our everyday life, people face problems like remembering too many numbers, too many names, and too many notes. Memory methods can solve this problem by using various mnemonic systems. Here is how you can have a better time remembering names and faces of people.

REMEMBERING NUMBERS: Remembering numbers is a crucial skill. We have to remember different codes, phone numbers, addresses, important events, appointments, passwords, etc. To remember numbers, we can think the number regarding figures. To do this, you must attach each number from 0 to 9 with a symbolic shape. For instance, the shape of an hourglass may suggest the number 8. Likewise, we attach other numbers with various objects. Now to remember any number we just cipher numbers into peg objects and compare these pegged objects with one another.

For instance, create a number shape system with numbers attached to various objects like the example below. You can use this sample or create one of your own:

The number 0 will peg to a football

The number 1 will peg to a candle

The number 2 will peg to a swan

The number 3 will peg to a butterfly

The number 4 will peg to a sailboat sail

The number 5 will peg to a hook

The number 6 will peg to an elephant's truck

The number 7 will peg to a hatchet

The number 8 will peg to an hourglass

The number 9 will peg to a tennis racket

Now, let's say you want to remember a shopping list:

(One) Eggs

(Two) Notebook

(Three) Chicken

The first thing you want to buy is eggs. Imagine yourself throwing a football at a shelf filled with eggs. Once the football hits, the eggs come cracking all over the floor.

The next thing you want to buy is a notebook. Imagine the notebook belonging to a person you don't admire. Set the notebook on fire with this candle. Continue in this manner for each of the items on your shopping list.

When you recall the shopping list, just begin with the number 0 and recall the associated number shape (here a football). This will bring back the memory of the football cracking the eggs on the floor and remind you that you need to buy eggs. Continue to do this practice for every number list.

REMEMBERING NAMES: Remembering names is an important skill for all people, especially if you are a teacher, doctor, lawyer, student, businessman, etc. Sometimes forgetting a name can place you in an embarrassing situation. The first rule for remembering the name is to be mindful and be present at the current moment. Put your entire focus on the person you are speaking with. When they announce your name, repeat it aloud in a relaxed manner such as, "Pleased to meet you, Sarah." And now link this person with all the people you already know with this name. For instance, picture all the Sarah's you know engaging in conversation with other people named Sarah. Also, correlate Sarah with the place where you are most likely to meet them again. Now associate all the Sarah's with a person or meaning. For instance, now see all Sarah (including the newly meet Sarah) shaking hands with someone famous like Sarah Palin or Sarah Silverman.

REMEMBERING FACES: Now to connect a name with a face, just try to imagine her face converting to pegged character. Watch him converting to Sarah Palin or overlap both faces. Also, notice the most prominent features on Paul's face and peg it with an image. For instance, her puffy cheeks can be imagined as fluffy clouds or a pillow. Now associate this image with a pegged character and likely place of meeting.

CHAPTER 8: BEATING PROCRASTINATION

Everyone has put off a task or an event at some point in their life. For instance, you may have planned to read this book earlier this week, but instead, you are just now reading it. But have you ever pondered why you or others procrastinate? While some people consider it as natural laziness, here are some likely reasons why tons of people procrastinate:

A GENERAL FEAR OF FAILURE: It is natural and normal to fear failure. Nevertheless, no one out of their right mind wants to fail in any area of their life. Some of us are better at recovering from failure than others. For instance, it is refreshing to know that you never begin on dinner rather than ruining the meal. But this train of thought is entirely negative and pessimistic! Failure is just a learning encounter for improving oneself. For those who fear failure, procrastination is a way not to chase any of their aspirations. Most people prefer handling this fear of not even attempting rather than trying to resolve this fear of failure. Living with a general fear of failure must come to resolve, but procrastinating is not the answer.

UNAPPEALING TASKS: If you have a number of tasks that are unappealing, you will procrastinate. Many people will rather do tasks that are gratifying and enjoyable while procrastinating on tasks that are less pleasant. Not all your tasks will be pleasant, but they still need to be completed, try implementing a reward system for the achievement of a tedious task.

MIND DISTORMENT: If you lack in clarity, it can make you prone to procrastinate. People who procrastinate are those that need a sense of focus or purpose in their lives. They are questionable in the sense of direction or are hesitant on how to overcome their circumstances. If you do not have a sense of purpose or a goal you someday you want to reach, you are bound to become a procrastinator. If you establish significant goals and a plan of action, it will help keep your focus and assist you in killing procrastination.

DISTRACTIONS: Your surrounding distractions is probably one of the primary cause we often procrastinate. The enticement to engage in chats, social media, video games, or other unprofessional activities can be sources of procrastination. To end your distractions – arrange your work area to minimize distractions and plan time to enjoy the fun and enjoyable activities. This will help evade procrastination and keep your life on track.

A FEELING OF UNMOTIVE: If you lack in mental or physical energy and feel apathetic, this can be partially responsible for your procrastinating routines. It is crucial that place yourself in a healthy lifestyle that encourages healthy foods, healthy sleep, and healthy exercise to maintain a healthy physical body, a healthy mind, and a healthy soul.

When you feel fatigued or unexcited, how can you possibly be productive? This can contribute to how productive you are. People who are always zealous about what they do will effortlessly finish their task in a matter of seconds.

PERFECTIONISM: Perfectionism is a normal cause on why people procrastinate. People want everything to be in absolute perfection before they ever begin working. But perfectionism can affect our self-confidence, productivity, self-esteem, and even our physical well-beings. Obsessing over perfection will make you run off course until you feel satisfied with achieving the desired outcome.

While there is nothing immoral about craving perfection, but if it becomes a constant effort, then it is a dilemma that needs to be resolved. If perfection is restraining you from commencing, then it can do you no good. It is better to be imperfect but can complete your task when needed. Perfection could hinder your course to success more than you would like. Thriving for perfection implies you lack compassion for oneself. Once you accept the fact that perfection is inevitable, you will find the incentive and liveliness to finish your everyday duties.

If you are battling against procrastination and putting things off, try any of these tips to put you back on course:

COMPLETE YOUR TASKS AS SOON AS YOU GET THEM: You need to get back to a client, what do you do? Do you come up with reasons to not answer them until the next time around? Do you answer them the minute you have the chance? Once you start your duties pronto, it preserves you the precious time on doing stuff later. When you have something you need to do, don't tell yourself to do it later. Tell yourself to do it right now at this very moment!

CHUNK DOWN YOUR DUTIES: One of the most prominent reasons why people procrastinate is because they are exhausted and overwhelmed by the many duties that they must perform. When you have a heavy workload, it's too easy to stress, get distracted, get unmotivated, and lose focus. People will often contemplate of how it is impossible to finish and why they should give up now. As a way to resolve this problem, break down your tasks into tiny and manageable pieces. Break down your major work into simple, specific, and easy tasks. This will make it much easier for you to keep track of your progress and allow you to manage them one after another.

START WITH THE HARD STUFF: While it is way laid-back with easy assignments, it will be more advantageous to finish the most horrendous of projects out of your way. The quicker you finish the difficult tasks, the faster you can put them out of your way. Since these tasks continue to remain on your activity list, the likelihood for you procrastinate increases because these are the things that you don't want to do. When you finish them quickly, you put your mind at ease and become more stress-free, making it easier for you to focus and be productive.

APPRECIATE IMPERFECTIONISM: Many procrastinators procrastinate because they work very hard to be perfect when in fact, it's impossible. No man nor woman is perfect. People will spend time making things perfect rather than starting and finishing their tasks and accepting the imperfections and mistakes along the way. Whether it's consciously or unconsciously, perfectionists will always look for a defect and fix it until the closing minute. You need to abandon perfectionism and accept the fact that no matter how much time you waste on your tasks, it cannot be perfect, there's destined to be mistaken. Once you do this, you will observe a significant difference in your productivity.

STOP NERVE-WRACKING ABOUT THE FUTURE: Keep your mind keen onto the present moment and what you need to get started on right now instead of being worried about the future. Set your mind to the first thing that needs to be completed and clear your brain of any other distractions. Don't think about what you will do after, don't think about taking a break. This will improve your focus on your tasks and allow you to move speedily through them.

STAY OPTIMISTIC: When you begin your day off with positivity, it leads to more positive events during your day to occur. Every morning initiate positivity and love. Remind yourself that today will be the most productive day you ever experience. Doing this will make you more productive whether you are consciously or subconsciously aware of it. Even if your day comes as unproductive - never lose sight! Keep feeding yourself with positivity, and you will be destined for productivity and the best in your life. You will be able to finish your to-do list without dreading it.

DON'T OVERCOMPLICATE TASKS: When you are confronted with a chore, what do you tell yourself? Do you remind yourself on how to get started? Do you tell yourself when to get started? What are the things you need to begin? Whether this will help you in life or not? Many chronic procrastinators will waste too much precious time complicating very simple and easy tasks in order to find reasons on not to do it. To beat procrastinating, keep things simple. Be productive and never complicate anything.

MAKE A DETAILED TO-DO LISTS: Between our professional and personal lives, pursuing our ambitions, hanging with friends, and completing projects all seem mind-boggling to do in just one day. When you build a clear activity list, it will help you master your time and become more productive at work. Coming up with a bunch of to-do's forces, us to set concrete goals, which can be a way more effective than just thinking about unclear intentions. Additionally, making a written schedule can assist us in recalling information that we will mostly prevent procrastinating.

As you go through your day, check off all the completed tasks off your activity list. This way, you will provide a positive reassurance and a rewarding satisfaction as you see your list becoming shorter and shorter. Here is some advice in mind to make the most fruitful to do list:

KEEP A NOTEPAD. On this notepad, you will write down everything that needs to get done. If you ever are confused or run off course, all you need to do is check this mini-notepad. Always update this notepad every hour or two to fully mobilize your productivity.

MULTIPLE TO-DO LISTS When you have only a minuscule number of things you need to get done, it makes it easier and more convenient for you to complete them. For instance, make a to-do list for work, a to-do list for work, a to-do list for personal interests, etc. However, you should create one master list with everything that absolutely must be done today or for the long-term.

CREATE A DEADLINE FOR EACH INDIVIDUAL TO-DO-LISTS. Procrastinators will often come up with reasons to do things later. When you set a specific deadline to complete each task, it provides you more motivation to complete them.

TAKE A COUPLE OF MINUTES TO CHECK YOUR PROGRESS. As you carry on through your day, check your progress and see if you are ahead or behind of your to-do list, bring up-to-date your urgencies and make sure that you remain on course.

PRIORITIZE! Obviously, one of the best things to do on any to-do list is prioritized each activity with a level of urgency. Learn to prioritize and put your utmost attention on the most important tasks first. Pay attention and be stricter on the things you normally set aside.

Do not stress out over your to-do-list. If your activity list is filled with unpleasant duties and you are behind on your work, stressing out will not help. Try to figure out how long it will take to complete each task, take a breather, relax a little bit, and go back on finishing your list.

CHAPTER 9: VISUALIZATION TECHNIQUES FOR BETTER MEMORY

One way you can enhance your memory is by utilizing visualization techniques. In this section, you will learn how anticipating can provide you with a perfectly good and strong recognition. Utilizing visualizations means to imagine a mental image or scenario of something in your mind. Visualizations have the potential to make something more memorable and thought-provoking. These things will cling to your memory centers much more effective than your other five senses. Though, for effective visualizing, you will put to use all five senses.

Here are the fundamentals on visualizations:

To produce a conception all you need to do is shut your eyes and picture whatever you wish to see in your mind's eye. Easy as it sounds, right? However, it relies on how you are projecting this mental image or mental scenario.

Millions of individuals carry various representational systems, which means people encrypt information through their intellect by means of different senses as a foundation, whether it's your sense of smell, your sense of taste, your sense of touching, etc. If your main sense is your smell, listen, touch, or taste, you will have a challenging time conceiving visualizations. But do not worry too much, if that is your situation, you can strengthen your visualization efforts by continuous exercise.

Now to remember a memory or any sort of information, do your best to follow these guidelines:

TAKE IN AS MUCH SENSES AS YOU CAN WHEN YOU VISUALIZE. What do you see? What does it look like? Describe it in grave detail. What sounds can you hear? What smells can you smell? How does it feel pressing against your hand? What does it taste like? Never only use your sense of eyes. Rather make use of all five senses to make any kind of visualization as real as you can.

UTILIZE ACTION, MOVEMENT, AND ACTIVITY IN YOUR VISUALIZATIONS. Rather than just having plain mental images among your mind, mark how the fundamentals of the depiction cooperate between them. Make the illustrations move and allow a scenario to take place. After all, motion pictures are way better than bland images.

MAKE IT AS INTERESTING AS POSSIBLE. Your visualizations should be beautiful, fascinating, unusual, engaging, and captivating as much as you can conceive. Ask yourself: What alludes to me? The majority of people are attracted to beautiful and violent illustrations as it strikes our human sides. If you implement the things that appeal to you among your visualization, this will highly increase the likelihood of being retained.

So, let's put this into practice. Let's say that you need to evoke your boyfriend/girlfriend's birthday party tomorrow. To memorize it using visualization techniques, envision yourself at the birthday party already. What are you doing? What does it feel like? Who else is there? Picture your partner giving you a hug upon your arrival. Picture yourself singing happy birthday and about to enjoy a slice of cake. Picture yourself giving your partner a thoughtful gift. These images and scenarios will now stay in your memory for a lengthy amount of time.

TRAINING

To fully get maximize your talents in visualization, try to practice and indulge in these following exercises for the course of the week. It will only take five minutes, possibly less a day.

EXERCISE ONE: DAY ONE (MONDAY)

Pull up any image on your phone and examine every feature for precisely sixty seconds. Try to take in almost every detail as you possibly can. After sixty seconds, close your eyes and attempt to duplicate the exact image in your mind for three minutes or less. Do your best to retain as many features as you can.

EXERCISE 2: DAY TWO (TUESDAY)

Grip any item, whether it's a hardback novel, a plant, a kitchen utensil, or a mobile device. Examine it for exactly sixty seconds trying to take in as many features and details as you can for sixty seconds. After sixty seconds, close your eyes and attempt to duplicate the same figure in your head. Use your senses. Does it make any sound? What does it taste like? How does it feel? What does it look like? Ask yourself these questions and more to further boost this replication.

EXERCISE 3: DAY THREE (WEDNESDAY)

Examine the environment you are now. Absorb as many details as you can for exactly sixty seconds. After one minute, shut your eyes and try to duplicate this environment in your mind. Try to implant as many features and details as you possibly can. After a while, open your eyes and examine your environment again. See what you miss or what you added more of.

EXERCISE 4: DAY FOUR (THURSDAY)

Examine the environment you are now for exactly one minute. After one minute, close your eyes and reproduce the same environment in your mind. But this time, put yourself in this environment. Envision yourself in this room interacting with the objects around. Use all your sense interacting with your environment. What does it smell like? What does it feel like? What does it sound like? Continue to ask yourself these questions to further enhance this duplication.

EXERCISE 5: DAY FIVE (FRIDAY)

Inspect the environment you are in for sixty seconds. After sixty seconds, close your eyes and replicate the exact setting in your mind, including yourself in this setting. But this time, using your creative mind, implement amazing and wonderful things and features that you can interact with. For instance, add dragons, zombies, superheroes, a ton of money, etc. Ask yourself the same questions: What does it smell like? What does it feel like? What are you doing? What does it sound like?

Now with all these visualization practices at your dispense, you must remain practicing till you develop your visualization skills. With visualizations, it can serve as the foundation form memorizing things. For instance, you can utilize it to remember names, information, data, lists, dates, items, phone numbers, addresses, and so much more!

CHAPTER 10: HOW TO DOUBLE YOUR LEARNING SPEED

The key to enriching your memory retention and cognitive performance is the countless hours we spent developing it. However, the style in which we practice, in agreement with recent research has been proven oppositely. Researchers imply that by somewhat altering your learning style, you can sustain your brain more hard-working through the learning procedure, and cut off the time it needs to get up and to move to the regular model.

This research opposes the old-fashioned concept that repetition will make you learn things faster and memorize things effectively. While this is valid, there is a more productive way of doing so.

Every now and then you might be overwhelmed with the volume of information pressing against your brain. Even as you practice or teach, it can still feel like you are being bombarded with information, details, and data occasionally. What if you could overcome this and double your learning speed? In this chapter, you discover how you can amplify your learning speed dramatically.

Nonetheless, in this hectic society, how can we feasibly find the time to master new skills, acquire new knowledge, or enhance our memory when there is an endless list of things on our to-do lists? Here are some ways you can speed up your learning procedure and dramatically get things done.

INSTRUCT OR PORTRAY TO INSTRUCT SOMEONE. When you imagine yourself instructing someone else the things you are trying to grasp, you can further your learning abilities and retain more. Your goal shifts your thinking patterns so that you can engross in more practical approaches to learning than those who solely learn to ace an examination or to acquire the interests of others.

When instructors or supervisors try to explain something, they look for key points and organize instructions into an understandable structure. This also works for anyone else trying or pretending to explain to someone. This thinking pattern applies to anyone giving instructions.

Think about it for a second. You will comprehend more if you act like you are teaching others rather than cramming information at the last second. This will also trick your subconscious into believing you are an expert on the subject at hand – furthering your cognitive process

So, the next time you find yourself studying and just can't get the full picture all the way. Find a family member or friend you can explain it to. Or pretend to explain it back to yourself.

SEEK OUTSIDE YOUR EXPERTISE. If you are attempting to learn how to design a WordPress theme with absolutely some to none experience, it's going to take an extremely long time to learn. If you are trying to do something you are strange with, it is going to take longer to learn. The key to learning twice as fast is not having challenges with the subject at hand. For instance, a Photoshop expert can still use Photoshop after it underwent a major update without barely learning anything new. Why? Because the expert is already adapted to the subject at hand.

To learn something to the full extent, you must start small and build your expertise around the topic at hand. You must learn the fundamentals to become a master. This will make the process of learning way simpler, way quicker, and convenient for you to comprehend because you are constructing the knowledge you lack.

Strive to learn something new and exotic each day. Oprah Winfrey, Bill Gates, Warren Buffet and countless more exploit a five-hour. The five-hour rule is where an individual commits at least five hours each week for intentional learning. You should thrive to spend at least one hour each day to learn something new for the betterment of oneself. How about reading informational articles and blog posts? How about getting started on a novel? Expanding your vocabulary in another language? How about taking the advice from your mentors?

EXPERIMENT ON NEW THINGS. As it is essential to have the expertise to deal with challenges, those challenges must also be thought-provoking and out of this world for you to upgrade and truly become better. Research has proven that our minds are greater equipped and have a greater response to bizarre experiences than those that are foreseen.

When something comes as a habit, we can grasp it with our hands, but we won't feel enthusiastic about the process. When you focus on learning something that moves and amazes you, it will boost your odds in achieving peak performance.

LEARN IN TINY PIECES OF TIME. You should commit at least thirty-minutes a day to deliberate learning of the raw academic material. When you try to learn fewer than thirty minutes, it's not effective enough. However, when you learn for more than one hour, it can be entirely too exhausting for your brain to process in one session.

To utilize your cognitive abilities, you should take a break every five or ten minutes before you embark another studying or learning session. Temporary, intermittent learning sessions are deemed much more effective than lengthy, irregular ones.

Make some time for short learning sessions. Write notes by hand for the most troubling concepts and theories you are trying to comprehend. You never know when you will have an opportunity to take leverage of to learn!

CHAPTER 11: HOW TO MEMORIZE YOUR SPEECH OR PRESENTATION IN 60 MINUTES OR LESS

Whatever your vocation or line of work may be, you will undoubtedly find yourself speaking to a bulky audience at some point in time. Believe me. This will utterly happen. Maybe just right next week or a year from now. Hence, it's crucial that you memorize your presentation to regulate with others.

Whether you are a spokesman, a motivational speaker, a football coach, a businessperson, a chief executive officer, a politician, an employee, or just a mere college student, you are unavailable and have serious obligations to work on rather than memorizing a mere presentation. To comfort your mind a little bit, some of the best and influential presentations and speeches in history were never learned word for word, but learned.

It is unmissable when someone is talking from memory, rather than speaking from the heart about a topic you know comprehensively. Ponder about it for a second. A presentation or speech is intriguing when the speaker naturally understands what they are talking about rather than reading word for word. Why is this so? This is because when you present a speech you know in all directions, you will sound more engaged. There will be more emphasis on your words, and you will not be gawking at your notes, so you are interacting with the crowd by making eye contact. You will be a much better and effective communicator than someone who is rambling on learned by heart texts.

Here are some convenient tips and advice on how to memorize your speech or presentation under a crampy schedule or in less than an hour:

STEP 1: COMMENCE WITH A FRAMEWORK OF YOUR PRESENTATION OR SPEECH. When you attempt to memorize pages and pages of notes, which is unattainable for the majority of people in just a small amount of time, it will make your overall speech and presentation dulling and corny. Rather, perpetuate yourself to learning the outline or framework of the presentation! When you are writing your speech, never ever write it word for word! When you practice for your speech, never remember it word for word. Devote yourself to learning the major matters of your narrative, the most popular kind of framework is:

1. Introduction
2. Supporting Point One
3. Supporting Point Two
4. Supporting Point Three

5. Conclusion

For more business or professional suggestions, the typical framework is:

1. Identify and define the problem

2. Present the solution

3. How this will be for our benefit 1

4. How this will be for our benefit 2

5. Call to Action

Once you learn by heart your outlines, you can put all your understandings on the subject into creation. You can deliberate the major points you have premeditated and give details on these matters – and attach these subjects with a theme, a story, real-life examples, scientific research, and quotes. This will make your speech way more impactful, natural-sounding, and way more meaningful.

STEP 2: MOBILIZE MENTAL IMAGES FOR EVERY MAJOR POINT. This measure is a strong approach if you have difficulties with short-term memory loss or you always misremember a particular portion of your speech. Through this step, you will find specific sections of your speech and envision a scene or object that associates it.

As an illustration, if you are giving a speech on healthy eating, don't memorize word for word - try to imagine healthy fruits and vegetables. Why is this more efficient you may be asking? Because it's easier to remember images and motion pictures than words. For instance, you are likely to remember any theatrical scene from any Harry Potter movie than remembering an entire paragraph from the book.

Now, the next time you are rehearsing your speech and get stuck in a rut again. You will conceive images of healthy vegetables and fruits in your mind, and that's where your brain will start putting it together. Making it easier for you to go advance in your presentation.

This step will make it much easier and quicker for you to prepare for your speech as you will recall mental images and not words. To help get you started, here are some mental images connected to specific points that you are free to use:

When you are discussing an increase in profits, picture hundreds and hundreds of dollars piling up.

When you are discussing managing time, think of a clock or an hourglass.

When you are discussing communication, think of a telephone ringing or two people interacting with one another.

When you are discussing education or learning, think of books or a graduation cap.

When you are discussing goals, picture a trophy or a finished line.

When you are discussing rewards, think of a present, or one of your favorite treats, or even an Academy-Award winning trophy.

When you are discussing working smarter, not harder, picture a brain or a light bulb.

When you are discussing teamwork and getting along with one another, picture a football team huddling up.

STEP 3: USE A MEMORY PALACE. To memorize your speech or practically anything, you need a place to store the information. For a speech, you can use a mind palace. It's where you imagine what you want to remember on objects in a location. To do this, pick a location that you can remember in grave detail, it can be your bedroom, a park, your workplace, a kitchen, or even something made up. Come up with a tour of the room, depending on which objects you notice first. For instance, what are the things you see on tour from the entrance of your kitchen to your refrigerator?

Once you are done forming the tour, envision yourself taking this kitchen tour and focusing on the items in the order you observe them. In this example, when you enter your kitchen, you notice your kitchen counters and a microwave on top, right next to the microwave is your stove, and right next to the stove are some more counters and then your sink. Next to the sink is your refrigerator.

Now you can combine both your outline of your presentation to make the mental connection with objects in your memory palace. Do not worry if the connections are bizarre or unconventional, as that will aid you in remembering them quicker. The major point is that the object and subject connection are in the same sequential order as the items you see in the memory palace tour.

STEP 5: REVIEW AND PRACTICE. Review these objects and pictures over and over in your head until you fully grasp them. Rehearse the speech at least once from memory to make sure the images work for you. Once you become proficient with these methods, you could give a speech that lasts for hours without any notes at all.

Become flowing with your speech's outline and image connections. Then, when you get up in front of the crowd, you won't be sweating over what needs to be said. All you need to do is picture those objects, which present your points inside a location. The only thing you have left to do is visualize yourself getting up on stage, ready to give a powerful speech.

CHAPTER 12: HOW TO BECOME A SPEED READER

Contemplate about the numerous hours you can preserve if you learn how to improve your reading speed and perception. Learning how to speed read can place you in a huge advantage in college and in your vocation. The standard person reads at approximately two hundred to three hundred words per minute. If they maintain at this pace, a 250 to 300-page book will take them around six or eight hours to complete.

However, if you boost your reading pace, you'll be capable of comprehension in any lengthy paperback in a matter of three hours or less.

Now, take a moment to contemplate on all the studying and reading you do each day, whether in books, stories, reviews, blog posts, and articles, coursework, and even lengthy Facebook posts and YouTube comments. Once you choose to invest your time on obtaining speed reading attributes, you will save the loads amount of valuable time to read and study even more! Speed reading is a must-have skill that you cannot pass up – and here, you will discover how you can hasten your reading pace.

An undergraduate once asked Bill Gates what kind of superpower he most desired. And guess what? Bill Gates choose to be capable of reading lighting fast. Tons of successful people read all the time; some even read two or more books a week.

Besides the common benefit of preserving precious time, becoming a speed reader will allow you to read and study with additional time and with more passion! This can provide you a massive advantage.

And against to widespread belief, it's not required to be born a prodigy to learn how to flip through book after book. So many people view themselves as slow readers and believe that there is nothing in their authority to change that. However, they can! We are humanely capable of reading very, very fast!

The fundamental point about speed reading has nothing to do with superhuman abilities, but has everything to do with your perception and habituating your mind to be able to examine terms and data quicker.

It's a super easy and simple proficiency to comprehend, but one that little people ever commit to. Here is how you can boost your reading pace and become a lightning-fast speed reader:

FIGURE OUT YOUR PREVAILING READINGPACE: your basic reading pace is the pace whereupon you presently read. To calculate this amount, you will need to count the number of words for each line (in a textbook or such). Figure out how many texts are in five lines and divide the sum with five to acquire the average number (or mean) of words per line.

Do the exact thing by calculating the number of words in each line on five different pages. Then, divide this amount by five to acquire the average total of lines per page. Round the figure to the whole closet number.

Then, multiply the average number (or mean) of lines per page by the average number (or mean) of words per line to acquire the number of texts per page. Write down these numbers in a notebook for future citation. This shouldn't be too complicated.

Now, after you jot down those figures, choose a place to start reading and set a timer to exactly sixty seconds. Read from the base until the timer goes off, then figure out the total number of lines you read. Multiply the number by the average number (or means) of words per line to acquire your current reading speed.

REDUCE OR ELIMINATE SUBVOCALIZATION: Subvocalization, or some times recognized as auditory reassurance, is the indistinct voice you hear in your brain whenever you read something. Most people carry this annoying habit where they will speak each word in their heads whenever they are reading, even when they're not reading aloud.

When you do this, your reading rate will resolute by how fast you can talk. It is one of the primary reasons why most people read at a slow pace and have difficulty doubling their reading speed. Getting rid of or reducing subvocalization is the key to reading fast. However, it is the most difficult to learn.

To help get you started, study the words and their meaning without uttering the words. It will come off as outlandish and peculiar in the beginning, but your brain has already examined the majority of the words tons of times.

You won't ever need to expend the precious time speaking each word individually to realize their significance. You only need to develop your brain to be able to convert it quicker.

USE YOUR FINGERS AS A BOOK STICK: When you read without utilizing book pointers, this makes it likely for your eyes to stray away. What many people don't understand is, that they make extremely slight movements that require several milliseconds to regulate.

For when you use a book pointer, it enables your eyes to uphold better concentration to the details your brain is processing and empowers you to read quicker – this is also an excellent method for diminishing and eradicating subvocalization. Just for practice, use your index finger to bounce yourself to read one line per second.

As you sustain to read, mobilize your eyes to trail the words your index finger is on. You do need to be concern about understanding what you are reading. The goal of this method is to prepare your eyes to maneuver at the equivalent pace of your index finger. Retaining the details and information you read will come later on.

TAKE ADVANTAGE OF YOUR PERIPHERAL VISION: While many individuals read text for text, they as well read from the initial to the preceding word of each line. As you remain to teach your vision to hastily browse over words and understand their origins without mentally conveying them in your head, you can also teach your vision to focus on the central of the line and allow your peripheral vision to do the remainder of the work.

When you mobilize this method, you read scarcer words for every line and greatly boost your reading velocity.

To practice this aptitude, employ your index finger to measure yourself at one line for every second. However, pass over the primary and preceding word of each line, scan through the book for one minute. Don't concern yourself with retaining what you read or understanding what you read. Just keep your brain mentally sharp.

Keep on practicing this procedure over and over again. However, this time you will go over the first and final TWO words for another TWO minutes. Repeat once more, bouncing the first and last THREE words of each line and reading at the swiftness of one line for every point-five second. Just as a reminder, do not fret about retaining what you read. Just focus on the pace and procedure. Keep on practicing until you obtain the grip of it.

CHECK ON YOUR PROGRESS: After spending some time practicing and harnessing these routines, you are ready to read comprehensively. To achieve this, choose a basis in a book and read for precisely sixty seconds as hastily and as comprehensively as you can, while at the same time executing the methods you just learned.

You will observe how quickly you can read than usual and still hold all the details you read. When the timer beeps, calculate the quantity of lines you read and multiply it by the average amount (or mean) of words per line to unravel your newfangled words per minute rate. You will be quite impressed with the results.

If you can invest a mere ten minutes of your day for seven days to drill these methods to perfection, I guarantee you that you will likely become a speed reader. Like any other ability or body muscle, the more you train, the better you will get.

CHAPTER 13: INCREASING PRODUCTIVITY AND USING YOUR PHOTOGRAPHIC MEMORY FOR SUCCESS

You are only as productive as you crave to be. After all, it's a popular belief to think that being productive simply means working harder. On the other hand, being productive is all about the central idea of working smarter.

To really get your photographic memory on gears, you should devote on becoming a productivity master. Now for certain people, it may take them all day for them to complete their to-dos. For other people, it may take them mere hours before they get all their to-dos out of their way. And for most of us, our daily to-do lists may span across the seven-day week.

In this section, you will find how you can become more productive in your endeavors. This chapter will certainly help you as a student, teacher, lawyers, translators, accountants, etc.

Everything you read is quite simple, easy, and effective. However, it requires patience, commitment, and effort to ingrain them permanently in our lives.

KICKOFF YOUR DAY VERY EARLY: When you start your day very early in the morning, you provide yourself with enough time to prepare for your day with little commotions. Early mornings tend to be the most productive time of the day, and this can help kick-start on all your tasks. And a fresh start usually keeps you driven for the rest of your day.

The very moment you wake up, you can spend time either meditating, exercising, playing brain boosting games, eating a healthy nutritious breakfast, reading affirmations, or writing in your gratitude journal. It also can help refresh your memory by recalling all the material you need for advancement.

FIND THE MOTIVATION BEHIND YOUR ACTIONS: Figure out why you do the things you do. What is yours why? If you can't think of any. Come up with as many reasons on why you need to be productive and why you need to enhance your memory. Most people say they desire career advancement and promotions or that they want to stop overlooking things.

Think of the after effects and what would happen if you just give up. Once you establish a sense of purpose, it can help you focus even better and retain information quickly. And in return, this can help gain better results!

Ask yourself thought-provoking questions: What are you trying to do? Why do you want to develop your memory? How will it serve you? How will a better memory make you more productive?

CARRY A NOTEBOOK WITH YOU MOST OF THE DAY: This simple method for being productive is one of the most effective. When you carry a journal with you, you can jot down any notes, any feelings, your to-dos, and anything else you deem important. You can write down as many important notes and figures. One advantage of having a notebook with you is that you are able to refer to this notebook whenever you misremember something.

TAKE A BREAK NOW AND THEN: Throughout your day, you may carry loads of stress from all the responsibilities and exercises you indulge in. For instance, it may be overwhelming if you have hundreds of tasks on your to-do-list. It is best to take breaks after completing a few tasks or so.

This also can help you feel more compelled to finish your tasks because you will treat your breaks as a reward system or such.

REMOVE ANY DISTRACTIONS: When you are continuously receiving notifications from your phones, laptops, and from other devices, it can be alluring to check them all out. One solution to this problem is to cut out all sorts of distractions by getting rid of all non-essential sounds while you are working on something important or studying for an upcoming quiz.

Do everything in your power to stay attune and on course because otherwise the things you need to get done won't be done on time and with quality.

WRITE AN NOT-TO-DO LIST: While the classic to-do-lists are productive and useful, a not-to-do list will provide you with all the things you should not (or never) do. A not-to-do list will overcome procrastination and will not place you under overwhelming pressure on time wasting activities. Here are a few things you should consider writing on your not-to-do list:

Do not check your emails the first thing in the morning.

Do not check your emails the last thing at night.

Do not agree to conferences without a clear scheme or end time.

Do not multitask.

Do not let people rant or ramble on in the conversation.

Do not keep your phone on you 24/7.

Do not look for a cheaper way to do something.

Do not watch television or YouTube videos for endless hours.

Do not try to become perfect.

Do not allow your apps and messages to keep notifying you.

Do not compare yourself with other people's skills and performance.

Do not become unmotivated after negative feedback or an uneventful experience.

CONCLUSION

Your memory operates on its own free will, but it's still a necessary ingredient for a healthy life. By attempting to improve your memory, you will support both your mind and body to work in concurrently with one another. You will not only become more productive and successful, but you'll also feel satisfied and happy with all the beneficial things you've memorized with comfort, as averse to being disappointed over many things which you would usually forget because of a bad memory.

Your memory is always something for improvement and nothing you should take for granted. Take advantage of each day to develop your mind, your brain, and your memory!

In this book, you have access to the materials needed to become more productive, learn faster, and amass greater success in your life. You should continue to thrive and practice every day, and by doing this, you will keep your brain healthy and in well-condition. The question is: How committed are you to exercise and make positive changes in your life to obtain the best of memory?

Create a course of action to the distinct approaches that you can review these techniques to improve your memory, and then go to work and put them into action. Pick any of these methods and begin exercising them right away. To keep from growing fatigued, raise the level of difficulty in the memory by carrying out various sorts of challenges and advancements. The course of action you make now to improve your memory will benefit you for an entire lifetime

To bring down the curtain, I want to ensure you that you can surely master and improve your memory to the utmost. You have the power to improve memory and use it to your benefit at all powers. All you need is willpower, self-discipline and the tips contained in this book to better your memory and to bring success in your educational, professional, and personal pursuits. Many people believe that there's no reason for people to improve our memory, but they're wrong. With repetition and consistent practice, you can use a better memory to master any skill, ace any tests, pursue your ambitions, and become more successful in life. Even if you do find it getting rough, don't give up!

Lastly, if you enjoyed this book, please take the time to review it on Amazon. Your honest feedback would be greatly appreciated.

Thank you, and the best of blessings on your academic, professional and personal journey!

Thank you!

Thank you for downloading this book. I hope you found this book interesting and advices was helpful for you.

Please feel free to leave your honest review about my book here:

https://www.amazon.com/review/create-review/133-1279912-1108151?ie=UTF8&asin=B074NBF95T&channel=glance-detail&ref_=cm_cr_dp_d_wr_but_top&#

Printed in Great Britain
by Amazon